Symbols and Society

Symbols and Society

Essays on Belief Systems in Action

CAROLE E. HILL, EDITOR

Southern Anthropological Society
Proceedings, No. 9

SOUTHERN ANTHROPOLOGICAL SOCIETY
Distributed by the University of Georgia Press
Athens 30602

Southern Anthropological Society

Founded 1966

To
Frank J. Essene

Contents

Preface

In dedicating this volume to Frank J. Essene, we express not only our appreciation, but also our intent—his move to the Northwest notwithstanding—to continue to draw upon the sound guidance he has provided the Society since he presided at its first meeting.

The ninth annual meeting of the Southern Anthropological Society was held on April 4-6, 1974, at Blacksburg, Va., hosted by the Virginia Polytechnic Institute and State University. We thank Joseph B. Aceves and Carole E. Hill, program coordinators, for the rich variety of topics covered in the sessions.

With some exceptions, the papers in this volume constituted the key symposium at the meeting. In adding the contributions by Clifford Geertz and Victor W. Turner, we acknowledge their authority in the subject of symbols and society.

Irma Honigmann
SAS Editor

Introduction: The Study of Beliefs and Behavior

Carole E. Hill

The study of beliefs and behavior has long been a topic of concern among anthropologists. On the one hand, the cognitive assumptions of individuals and groups are inextricably bound to observable behavioral patterns. At the same time, as Weber and others have reminded us, behavior cannot be fully understood without understanding the beliefs or subjective meanings that are assigned to behavior by individuals. The papers in this volume examine from a wide range of perspectives the interrelatedness of these two aspects of human life.

The study of beliefs and behavior has traditionally been framed within the domain of religion, and within that domain scholars have developed several approaches to deal with the relationship between religious beliefs and observable behavior. In the last century the historian Fustel de Coulanges (1963) influenced the development of a functionalist approach through demonstrating the integrative function of religion in other Greek and Roman institutions. He maintained that changes in the history of these people were due directly to changes in religious beliefs. Furthermore, the functionalist approach, particularly that of Durkheim and Radcliffe-Brown, views religion as maintaining social unity and stability in a society while explicitly assuming that beliefs reinforce the social structure. Even when dealing with social change, we find two exponents of this model, Gluckman (1954) and Turner (1966), attempting to demonstrate the reinforcing nature of beliefs and rituals. In his analysis of the Nuer, Evans-Pritchard (1953) exemplifies the functionalist approach in relating how their beliefs concerning spirits (supernatural order) are refracted or modeled on their social order. Horton, in his earlier writings, in fact defines religion as "an extension of the field of people's social relationships beyond the confines of human society" (1960:211). The emphasis of this approach, however, has been on observable behavior, focusing on ritual and on the functions of ritual in society. Somewhat similar is the social-psychological approach (Malinowski 1948) which emphasizes the function of religion in individual behavior and attempts to demonstrate that ritual functions to reduce anxiety and inspire confidence in man. Again, however, we find a major concern with ritual as such, with how ritual unifies society and affects the individual, rather than with a concern for beliefs. A few, more recent studies have utilized the Weberian model in analyzing the relationship between the religious system and other institutions in a society. These demonstrate the ways religious beliefs can stimulate social change (Bellah 1957; Geertz 1960). Here we find a stronger emphasis on belief than in the other approaches. However, all these approaches, in varying degrees, assume that a central function of beliefs is to provide explanations for happenings in the world in which people find themselves; they make sense out of the world.

A belief system is concerned with the schemes people construct to make sense out of their experiences and to order the universe. In other words, societies or social groups have a common core of beliefs that set parameters on expected behavior (Spiro 1966). A belief system involves the cognitive assumptions individuals in a society make about the nature of the world and ramifies throughout all of a society's institutions. The system of belief influences and regulates behavior in addition to validating behavioral systems and providing explanations for behavior. Thus, a belief system involves more than people's relations with the supernatural. It allows for a broader field of study than religion through examining political beliefs, economic beliefs, stratification beliefs, and the like, and relating them to behavior.

The papers in this volume link beliefs to many kinds of action.[1] Some papers remain within the religious belief system itself, relating ritual behavior to religious belief, while others go beyond religious belief and relate secular action to a wider system of beliefs. Hudson and Tooker, for example, examine ritual situations of two North American Indian tribes, Cherokee and Iroquois, and discuss the meaning these rituals have for the society in light of their worldview. Tooker uses an innovative approach to discuss ways in which the analysis of forms of ritual can provide a key to understanding the belief system (ethnometaphysics) of the Iroquois. Hudson focuses, in a similar manner, on one ritual of the Cherokee, vomiting, and examines various alternative explanations for this behavior within the framework of their belief system. Both these papers view ritual as a system of meaning that can have various explanations depending on the ritual situation and on the level of interpretation. These approaches are reminiscent of the work of Victor Turner (1966) in which he proposes three levels of interpretation of ritual: (1) external form and observable characteristics; (2) explanations of ritual given to the anthropologist by the people themselves (conscious beliefs), and (3) the anthropologist's construction of a system of meaning of symbols in ritual situations which are assumed to be on the unconscious level for the participants themselves.

Several papers analyze behavior in areas such as education, social mobility, and alcoholism in terms of the various beliefs systems operating in the society. They go beyond the traditional sacred or religious behavior and demonstrate the ways beliefs are actualized in a broad range of situations. Most of the papers relate various cosmologies to the outside world.[2] They are concerned with how the symbolic nature of these cosmologies are transmitted into sacred or secular action. This dialectical process is clearly presented in Peacock's analysis of Southern Baptists and Indonesian Muslims through the utilization of Weber's "ideal types." Peacock demonstrates the ways these groups form contrasting paradigms for action. Once the meaning of the basic symbols can be discerned, he argues, then these symbols can be correlated with behavior. For example, among the Southern Baptists, the meanings of symbols surrounding the conversion experience are made operational through changes in attitude and behavior for the individual. Using a similar model, Manning delineates the dominant symbols of the Seventh-day Adventists in the West Indies and then relates the meaning of these symbols to the group's behavior. Likewise, Turner[3] gives as an example the symbol system of a hunting ritual of the Ndembu and demonstrates that the meaning of ritual symbols becomes clearer in an action system. In addition, he argues that symbols are more than informational storage units; they are the crucial factors in social action.

The central focus of the volume, then, is on the belief system as an integrated intellectual system of meaning and symbols that can be studied in its own right rather than merely as a reflection or projection of social life. Appropriately, we begin the volume with a reprint of an article by Clifford Geertz in which he discusses the concept of ideology and focuses on the relationship between ideological attitudes and symbolic structures. Thus, we are dealing here with the "analysis of a system of meaning embodied in the symbols which make up the religion or the beliefs" (Geertz 1966:42). The central problem to which we address ourselves is the delineation of beliefs and symbols in articulation with behavior—how do beliefs translate into action?

It is assumed that there is some degree of fit between a belief system and a behavior system; however, when a society is undergoing social change, beliefs and action may fit imperfectly as Geertz (1966) demonstrates with a Javanese case. He states that "cultural integration [can] no longer be taken to be locked away from the common life of man in a logical world of its own . . . patterns counteractive to the primary ones exist as subdominant but nonetheless important themes" (1966:65-67). Earlier, in criticizing the functional approach for its inability to handle social change, Geertz (1957) distinguishes between culture and society. Culture is seen as "an ordered system of meaning and of symbols in terms of which social interaction takes place," and society "as the pattern of social interaction itself" (1957:33). Culture is "a framework of beliefs, expressive symbols and values in terms of which individuals define their world" (a logical-meaningful integration), and society is "the ongoing process of interactive behavior" (causal-functional integration) (1957:33-34). He then demonstrates how an incongruity can exist between the belief system and the behavior system due to a situation of change. Contrary to the traditional sociological approach, Geertz feels that in certain situations these two systems are not mere reflections of one another, but somewhat independent, yet interdependent variables.

Recognizing the theoretical problems posed by situations of change, Keesing and Keesing (1971:327) urge anthropological investigation into the extent to which an ideological system fits together with the social system. This, indeed, is a focus of the articles presented here. Perhaps through examining situations of change we can gain clearer insights into how belief systems are put into action and consequently can develop more powerful tools for understanding and explaining the nature of the interaction between the two systems.

Goodman's paper provides a new approach to this problem, utilizing transformational theory in linguistics. She relates how new transformational rules, not changes in the "cultural deep structure," account for shifts in behavior among an Indian group in Mexico. Angrosino selects a different approach, but one also dealing with social change. He demonstrates the process involved in actualizing beliefs in Trinidad, a society undergoing modernization. He examines the meaning of drinking in Trinidad in the context of two symbolic representations, reputation and respectability, and how Alcoholics Anonymous fits into and is responsive to the prevailing belief systems. His study demonstrates the relevance of understanding the beliefs of a particular group before undertaking planned change in its action systems. Similarly, Preston demonstrates discontinuity between cultural meanings and social behavior of the Cree. They have nevertheless incorporated the white man's beliefs and behavior into their traditional systems, thus providing themselves with a basis for innovation and change in Cree society.

We find, then, that particularly in complex societies, several systems of beliefs can exist and that, in situations of change, choices are made. The existence of alternative beliefs in a given society is a crucial variable for the openness or closedness of a belief system (Horton 1973). So, perhaps the *content* of beliefs is more important in dealing with behavior and alternative behavior patterns in a society than are the *processes* of thought. As societies undergo change more alternatives are presented to individuals, and the behavior patterns they select or reject thus can be an aid in understanding beliefs in action, a kind of situational analysis.

One of the major approaches in anthropology today dealing with processes of thought is that of Lévi-Strauss and the structuralists. With their emphasis on logical ordering of the universe, they attempt to explain how contradiction in a belief system can be resolved. Some of the papers presented here, and other studies as well, deal with contradictions that on the surface appear to the anthropologist to render a system illogical. Keesing and Keesing point out that "one of the remarkable things about the human animal is his ability to tolerate and operate with inconsistent and contradictory beliefs and customs" (1971:327). According to Lévi-Strauss (1963), it is myth in primitive societies that provides a logical model capable of overcoming contradictions, especially those between the intellectual system and the behavior system. The structural approach, however, is based on a linguistic model that has not produced an adequate explanatory level of analysis. In her paper Goodman, perhaps, provides a step forward by relating these systems more adequately, using another linguistic model that may prove to be a more powerful explanatory tool.

Contradictions on the action level or in the statements from informants often reveal the patterning on the belief level. Contradictions, then, although illogical to the anthropologist, have a function in a belief system. Hudson (1972) has suggested that contradiction can function to explain a wider range of events on the action level and thus allow for alternative behavior. Hill (forthcoming) has demonstrated how contradictions can not only explain a broader range of behavior but can also form a logical system if situational factors are taken into consideration. A similar approach has been advocated by Horton (1962) in a search for logical consistency in a belief system. He uses a hierarchy of models to explain contradictions in the belief system of the Kalabari. Horton (1970) takes what the people say "at face value" and feels that this "intellectualist approach" aids in explaining human behavior. He has later argued that by not taking traditional explanations at their face value, the anthropologist may be avoiding comparisons between different modes of thought and evading value judgments (Horton 1973:294). He makes clear, however, that the intellectualist approach should not be regarded as an alternative to the analysis of belief and behavior systems but as an important complement.

In the anthropological study of belief and behavior systems, several types of explanations relate beliefs to social organization. Five different approaches will be presented in summary fashion for comparative purposes.

Some anthropologists feel that explanation needs to be tied to the empirical level. The positivist approach of the functionalist is perhaps most representative of this model. Beliefs are not generally taken at their face value for building a system of belief and behavior. However, in order to understand as well as explain beliefs, it is necessary to consider the explanations of the behavior given by the people under study. What the anthropologist has to work with is observable behavior and what the people say about their lives. From this, the anthropologist attempts to construct a belief system that more or less reflects reality—an explanatory model.

One of the first monographs to document in detail the way people use a corpus of explanatory theory to make sense out of and cope with their everyday lives was written by Evans-Pritchard (1937). He showed how the Zande belief system explained unfortunate events in a logical manner, and he then related Zande beliefs to their social life. With this work, we have a model for actions and beliefs grounded in empiricism on a descriptive level.

Another approach stems from the social action theory of Weber, which utilizes ideal types to explain "meaningful social action." Weber tries to synthesize the positivist approach and the idealist approach to phenomena. To him, the aim of cultural science is to *understand,* and the method of understanding is the use of ideal types. Through constructing ideal types the anthropologist is better able to understand individual and group behavior. Ideal types are hypothetical individuals constructed by the anthropologist for the purpose of comparison. Thus, an ideal type is a strategy for empirical explanation. Weber also assumed that subjective meanings are a cause of behavior and that behavior cannot be understood without knowing the meaning behind the behavior. Many behaviors appear similar but can be interpreted very differently in terms of the meaning involved. This approach delineates not so much a logical structure as the interplay between symbols and society. Weber's classic study along these lines is his analysis of the rise of capitalism in Europe and its relation to the ideology of Protestantism

(1958). Victor Turner's analysis of Ndembu ritual symbols has some striking similarities to the Weberian approach. Although he does not use ideal types, Turner (1966) feels that the crucial properties of ritual symbols involve the processes of temporal change in social relations. He states that "symbols instigate social action. . . . In a field context they may even be described as 'forces' in that they are determinable influences inclining persons and groups to action" (1966:36). Thus, the action field context and the cultural (meaning) context have to be taken into consideration in understanding and explaining a symbol system.

Horton offers another type of analysis. He aims at explaining and understanding the belief system just as does the Weberian approach, but from a very different perspective. Horton analyzes the worldview of the Kalabari of the Niger Delta and postulates a hierarchy of models to explain their behavior. He states that "as we ascend from level to level, fewer and fewer of the categories appropriate to the description of observable reality apply" (1962:211). Furthermore, the Kalabari are not aware of the four-level structure of their belief system, but it is perceived by the anthropologist.

Lévi-Strauss's (1963) approach, the last presented here, aims to build a model of unconscious reality beginning with what the people of a culture say about their lives (conscious reality) and ending with the unconscious model constructed by the anthropologist which is the structure of their thought. This level cannot be reduced to social relations and is deduced through a series of logical steps. The final step comes when structures in several societies are deduced and compared in order to build a model of the structure of structures representing the essence of human thought.

Thus, each of the five approaches relating beliefs and behavior displays a different theoretical and philosophical orientation:

1. Model for action (functionalists)
2. Model for beliefs and action (Evans-Pritchard)
3. Model for beliefs and action (Weber and Turner)
4. Model for unconscious beliefs (Horton)
5. Model for unconscious processes of thought (Lévi-Strauss)

As we move from level to level, from functionalists to Lévi-Strauss, fewer and fewer of the categories appropriate to the description of observable reality apply. This is reminiscent of Horton's (1962) analogy between the Kalabari belief system and the levels of scientific explanation. At each progressive level, more powerful explanations of behavior emerge when we consider the beliefs, both conscious and unconscious, of people. Thus some approaches more than others view beliefs as constituting an important aspect in explaining and understanding behavior. The last two levels are more concerned with unconscious meaning and with constructing schemes to explain belief systems. This review should not be construed as all-inclusive but as a cursory look at selected approaches to the study of beliefs and behavior. In addition, the various levels are obviously not entirely mutually exclusive.

Since Geertz (1966:42) expressed his dissatisfaction with social anthropological work in religious beliefs, we find many recent studies analyzing belief systems. This once-neglected area of research is now expanding. Although the papers in this volume develop no single theoretical framework, they do present several creative approaches for studying the integration of belief and behavioral systems in human life.

Several of the authors view beliefs and behavior as two aspects of the same thing (religion). Consequently, the problem of relating belief systems to behavioral systems is not relevant to them. Others view beliefs and behavior as separate analytical systems and the connection between them becomes a critical question. These two divergent views reflected in the papers may be generated by the nature of the society under study. For example, in small-scale societies, much of people's behavior is "ritualized" due to the precariousness of their way of life (Beattie 1964:202-206). In more complex societies, the belief and behavior systems are more separated and thus behavior appears more secular.

Another main thread running through the articles deals with symbols and their meaning in society. The meaning of symbols can vary; for example, conversion symbolizes rebirth among the Southern Baptists (Peacock); vomiting symbolizes purity among the Cherokee (Hudson); drinking symbolizes respectability among the Hindus (Angrosino); and the Sabbath symbolizes law among West Indies Adventists (Manning); hunting cults symbolize masculine attributes and relationships of the family, on the one hand, and the tribal group, on the other, among the Ndembu (Turner). As David Sapir[4] pointed out, the symbol systems in these papers can be represented by several contrasting sets of meaning such as dramatistic/legalistic, flip-flop rule/gradual change, internal sin/external pollution, and open/elitist. Another related theme throughout the volume is a concern with the problem of how beliefs relate to action, especially in situations of change. Although the contributors utilize different approaches and interpretations to the central theme of beliefs in action, they all address themselves to the basic theoretical problems described here and ground their ideas in their own ethnographic research.

NOTES

Many people were indispensable to me in putting this volume together. My appreciation is extended to Nancy Collier and Judy Todd, who assisted me in the daily routine of handling the paper work. In addition, my thanks to William Coleman, Valerie Fennell, and Gwen Neville for their comments and suggestions. My sincere thanks is extended to Ernestine Friedl and David Sapir for their insightful discussions of the papers when they were presented orally at the 1974 annual Southern Anthropological Society meeting. And, finally, my appreciation to Irma Honigmann, Proceedings Editor, for her guidance and patience over the past year.

[1]The ideas in this paragraph stem from Ernestine Friedl's discussion of the papers.

[2]The ideas in this discussion stem from David Sapir's remarks about the papers.

[3]Although Turner did not participate in the key symposium, his original paper presented here was deemed an appropriate addition to the volume in that it deals with the central issues of the symposium.

[4]In his discussion of the papers.

REFERENCES

Beattie, John, 1964. *Other Cultures* (New York: Free Press).

Bellah, Robert N., 1957. *Tokugawa Religion: The Values of Pre-Industrial Japan* (Glencoe: Free Press).

Evans-Pritchard, E. E., 1937. *Witchcraft, Oracles and Magic among the Azande* (Oxford: Clarendon Press).

————, 1953. The Nuer Conception of Spirit in Its Relation to the Social Order. *American Anthropologist* 55:201-214.

Fustel de Coulanges, N. D., 1963. *The Ancient City* (New York: Doubleday). (First published in 1864.)

Geertz, Clifford, 1957. Ritual and Social Change: A Javanese Example. *American Anthropologist* 59:32-59.

————, 1960. *The Religion of Java* (Glencoe: Free Press).

————, 1966. Religion as a Cultural System. In *Anthropological Approaches to Religion,* Michael Banton, ed. (London: Tavistock Publications), pp. 1-46.

Gluckman, Max, 1954. *Rituals of Rebellion in Southeast Africa* (Manchester: Manchester University Press).

Hill, Carole E. A Folk Medical Belief System in the Rural South: Some Theoretical and Practical Considerations. In *Reader in Medical Anthropology,* David Evans, ed. (forthcoming).

Horton, Robin, 1960. A Definition of Religion and Its Uses. *Man* 90:201-226.

————, 1962. The Kalabari World-View: An Outline and Interpretation. *Africa* 32:197-219.

————, 1970. Neo-tylorianism: Sound Sense or Sinister Prejudice. *Africa* 40:625-634.

————, 1973. Lévy-Bruhl, Durkheim and the Scientific Revolution. In *Modes of Thought: Essays on Thinking in Western and Non-western Societies,* Robin Horton and Ruth Finnegan, eds. (London: Faber and Faber), pp. 249-305.

Hudson, Charles, 1972. The Structure of a Fundamentalist Christian Belief

System. In *Religion and the Solid South,* Samuel S. Hill, ed., (Nashville: Abingdon Press), pp. 122-142.

Keesing, Roger M., and Felix M. Keesing, 1971. *New Perspectives in Cultural Anthropology* (New York: Holt, Rinehart, and Winston).

Lévi-Strauss, Claude, 1963. The Structural Study of Myth. In *Structural Anthropology,* by Lévi-Strauss (New York: Basic Books).

Malinowski, Bronislaw, 1948. *Magic, Science and Religion, and Other Essays* (Boston: Beacon Press).

Spiro, Melford E., 1966. Religion: Problems of Definitions and Explanations. In *Anthropological Approaches to Religion,* Michael Banton, ed. (London: Tavistock Publications), pp. 85-126.

Turner, Victor, 1966. *The Forest of Symbols: Aspects of Ndembu Ritual* (Ithaca, N. Y.: Cornell University Press).

Weber, Max, 1958. *The Protestant Ethic and the Spirit of Capitalism* (New York: Scribner's).

Ideology as a Cultural System

Clifford Geertz*

THERE are currently two main approaches to the study of the social determinants of ideology: the interest theory and the strain theory (Sutton et al. 1956:11-12, 303-310). For the first, ideology is a mask and a weapon; for the second, a symptom and a remedy. In the interest theory, ideological pronouncements are seen against the background of a universal struggle for advantage; in the strain theory, against the background of a chronic effort to correct sociopsychological disequilibrium. In the one, men pursue power; in the other, they flee anxiety. As they may, of course, do both at the same time—and even one by means of the other—the two theories are not necessarily contradictory; but the strain theory (which arose in response to the empirical difficulties encountered by the interest theory), being less simplistic, is more penetrating, less concrete, more comprehensive.

The fundamentals of the interest theory are too well known to need review; developed to perfection of a sort by the Marxist tradition, they are now standard intellectual equipment of the man in the street, who is only too aware that in political argumentation it all comes down to whose ox is gored. The great advantage of the interest theory was and is its rooting of cultural idea-systems in the solid ground of social structure, through emphasis on the motivations of those who profess such systems and on the dependence of those motivations in turn upon social position, most especially social class. Further, the interest theory welded political speculation to political combat by pointing out that ideas are weapons and that an excellent way to institutionalize a particular view of reality—that of one's group, class, or party—is to capture political power and enforce it. These contributions are permanent; and if interest theory has not now the hegemony it once had, it is not so much because it has been proved wrong as because its theoretical apparatus turned out to be too rudimentary to cope with the complexity of the interaction among social, psychological, and cultural factors it itself uncovered. Rather like Newtonian mechanics, it has not been so much displaced by subsequent developments as absorbed into them.

The main defects of the interest theory are that its psychology is too anemic and its sociology too muscular. Lacking a developed analysis of motivation, it has been constantly forced to oscillate between a narrow and superficial utilitarianism that sees men as impelled by rational calculation of their consciously recognized personal advantage and a broader, but no less superficial, historicism that speaks with a studied vagueness of men's ideas as somehow "reflecting," "expressing," "corresponding to," "emerging from," or "conditioned by" their social commitments. Within such a framework, the analyst is faced with the choice of either revealing the thinness of his psychology by being so specific as to be thoroughly implausible or concealing the fact that he does not have any psychological theory at all by being so general as to be truistic. An argument that for professional soldiers "domestic [governmental] policies are important mainly as ways of retaining and enlarging the military establishment [because] that is their business; that is what they are trained for" seems to do scant justice to even so uncomplicated a mind as the military mind is reputed to be; while an argument that American oilmen "cannot very well be pure-and-simple oil men" because "their interests are such" that "they are also political men" is as enlightening as the theory . . . that the reason opium puts you to sleep is that it has dormitive powers.[1]

On the other hand, the view that social action is fundamentally an unending struggle for power leads to an unduly Machiavellian view of ideology as a form of higher cunning and, consequently, to a neglect of its broader, less dramatic social functions. The battlefield image of society as a clash of interests thinly disguised as a clash of principles turns attention away from the role that ideologies play in defining (or obscuring) social categories, stabilizing (or upsetting) social expectations, maintaining (or undermining) social norms, strengthening (or weakening) social consensus, relieving (or exacerbating) social tensions. Reducing ideology to a weapon in a *guerre de plume* gives to its analysis a warming air of militancy, but it also means reducing the intellectual compass within which such analysis may be conducted to the constricted realism of tactics and strategy. The intensity of interest theory is—to adapt a figure from Whitehead—but the reward of its narrowness.

As "interest," whatever its ambiguities, is at one and the same time a psychological and sociological concept—referring both to a felt advantage of an individual or group of individuals and to the objective structure of opportunity within which an individual or group moves—

so also is "strain," for it refers both to a state of personal tension and to a condition of societal dislocation. The difference is that with "strain" both the motivational background and the social structural context are more systematically portrayed, as are their relations with one another. It is, in fact, the addition of a developed conception of personality systems (basically Freudian), on the one hand, and of social systems (basically Durkheimian) on the other, and of their modes of interpenetration—the Parsonian addition—that transforms interest theory into strain theory.[2]

The clear and distinct idea from which strain theory departs is the chronic malintegration of society. No social arrangement is or can be completely successful in coping with the functional problems it inevitably faces. All are riddled with insoluble antinomies: between liberty and political order, stability and change, efficiency and humanity, precision and flexibility, and so forth. There are discontinuities between norms in different sectors of the society—the economy, the polity, the family, and so forth. There are discrepancies between goals within the different sectors—between the emphases on profit and productivity in business firms or between extending knowledge and disseminating it in universities, for example. And there are the contradictory role expectations of which so much has been made in recent American sociological literature on the foreman, the working wife, the artist, and the politician. Social friction is as pervasive as is mechanical friction—and as irremovable.

Further, this friction or social strain appears on the level of the individual personality—itself an inevitably malintegrated system of conflicting desires, archaic sentiments, and improvised defenses—as psychological strain. What is viewed collectively as structural inconsistency is felt individually as personal insecurity, for it is in the experience of the social actor that the imperfections of society and contradictions of character meet and exacerbate one another. But at the same time, the fact that both society and personality are, whatever their shortcomings, organized systems, rather than mere congeries of institutions or clusters of motives, means that the sociopsychological tensions they induce are also systematic, that the anxieties derived from social interaction have a form and order of their own. In the modern world at least, most men live lives of patterned desperation.

Ideological thought is, then, regarded as (one sort of) response to this desperation: "Ideology is a patterned reaction to the patterned strains of a social role" (Sutton et al. 1956:307-308). It provides a "symbolic outlet" for emotional disturbances generated by social disequilibrium. And as one can assume that such disturbances are, at least in a general way, common to all or most occupants of a given role or social position, so ideological reactions to the disturbances will tend to be similar, a similarity only reinforced by the presumed commonalities in "basic personality structure" among members of a particular culture, class, or occupational category. The model here is not military but medical: An ideology is a malady (Sutton et al. mention nail-chewing, alcoholism, psychosomatic disorders, and "crotchets" among the alternatives to it) and demands a diagnosis. "The concept of strain is not in itself an explanation of ideological patterns but a generalized label for the kinds of factors to look for in working out an explanation" (Parsons 1959b).

But there is more to diagnosis, either medical or sociological, than the identification of pertinent strains; one understands symptoms not merely etiologically but teleologically—in terms of the ways in which they act as mechanisms, however unavailing, for dealing with the disturbances that have generated them. Four main classes of explanation have been most frequently employed: the cathartic, the morale, the solidarity, and the advocatory. By the "cathartic explanation" is meant the venerable safety-valve or scapegoat theory. Emotional tension is drained off by being displaced onto symbolic enemies ("the Jews," "Big Business," "the Reds," and so forth). The explanation is as simple-minded as the device, but that, by providing legitimate objects of hostility (or, for that matter, of love), ideology may ease somewhat the pain of being a petty bureaucrat, a day laborer, or a small-town storekeeper is undeniable. By the "morale explanation" is meant the ability of an ideology to sustain individuals (or groups) in the face of chronic strain, either by denying it outright or by legitimizing it in terms of higher values. Both the struggling small businessman rehearsing his boundless confidence in the inevitable justness of the American system and the neglected artist attributing his failure to his maintenance of decent standards in a Philistine world are able, by such means, to get on with their work. Ideology bridges the emotional gap between things as they are and as one would have them be, thus insuring the performance of roles that might otherwise be abandoned in despair or apathy. By the "solidarity explanation" is meant the power of ideology to knit a social group or class together. To the extent that it exists, the unity of the labor movement, the business community, or the medical profession obviously rests to a significant degree on common ideological orientation; and the South would not be the South without the existence of popular symbols charged with the emotions of a pervasive social predicament. Finally, by the "advocatory explanation" is meant the action of ideologies (and ideologists) in articulating, however partially and indistinctly, the strains that impel them, thus forcing them into the public notice. "Ideologists state the problems for the larger society, take sides on the issues involved and 'present them in the court' of the ideological market place" (White 1961:204). Although ideological advocates (not altogether unlike their legal counterparts) tend as much to obscure as to clarify the true nature of the problems involved, they at least call attention to their existence and, by polarizing issues, make continued neglect more difficult. Without Marxist attack, there would have been no labor reform; without Black Muslims, no deliberate speed.

It is here, however, in the investigation of the social and psychological roles of ideology, as distinct from its determinants, that strain theory itself begins to creak and its superior incisiveness, in comparison with interest theory, to evaporate. The increased precision in the location of the springs of ideological concern does not, somehow, carry over into the discrimination of its consequences, where the analysis becomes, on the contrary, slack and ambiguous. The consequences envisaged, no doubt genuine enough in themselves, seem almost adventitious, the accidental by-products of an essentially nonrational, nearly automatic expressive process initially pointed in another direction— as when a man stubbing his toe cries an involuntary "ouch!" and incidentally vents his anger, signals his distress, and consoles himself with the sound of his own voice; or as when, caught in a subway crush, he issues a spontaneous "damn!" of frustration and, hearing similar oaths from others, gains a certain perverse sense of kinship with fellow sufferers.

This defect, of course, can be found in much of the functional analysis in the social sciences: A pattern of behavior shaped by a certain set of forces turns out, by a plausible but nevertheless mysterious coincidence, to serve ends but tenuously related to those forces. A group of primitives sets out, in all honesty, to pray for rain and ends by strengthening its social solidarity; a ward politician sets out to get or remain near the trough and ends by mediating between unassimilated immigrant groups and an impersonal governmental bureaucracy; an ideologist sets out to air his grievances and finds himself contributing, through the diversionary power of his illusions, to the continued viability of the very system that grieves him.

The concept of latent function is usually invoked to paper over this anomalous state of affairs, but it rather names the phenomenon (whose reality is not in question) than explains it; and the net result is that functional analyses—and not only those of ideology—remain hopelessly equivocal. The petty bureaucrat's anti-Semitism may indeed give him something to do with the bottled anger generated in him by constant toadying to those he considers his intellectual inferiors and so drain some of it away; but it may also simply increase his anger by providing him with something else about which to be impotently bitter. The neglected artist may better bear his popular failure by invoking the classical canons of his art; but such an invocation may so dramatize for him the gap between the possibilities of his environment and the demands of his vision as to make the game seem unworth the candle. Commonality of ideological perception may link men together, but it may also provide them, as the history of Marxian sectarianism demonstrates, with a vocabulary by means of which to explore more exquisitely the differences among them. The clash of ideologists may bring a social problem to public attention, but it may also charge it with such passion that any possibility of dealing with it rationally is precluded. Of all these possibilities, strain theorists are, of course, very well aware. Indeed they tend to stress negative outcomes and possibilities rather more than the positive, and they but rarely think of ideology as more than a *faute de mieux* stop-gap—like nail-chewing. But the main point is that, for all its subtlety in ferreting out the motives of ideological concern, strain theory's analysis of the consequences of such concern remains crude, vacillatory, and evasive. Diagnostically it is convincing; functionally it is not.

The reason for this weakness is the virtual absence in strain theory (or in interest theory either) of anything more than the most rudimentary conception of the processes of symbolic formulation. There is a good deal of talk about emotions "finding a symbolic outlet" or "becoming attached to appropriate symbols"—but very little idea of how the trick is really done. The link between the causes of ideology and its effects seems adventitious because the connecting element—the autonomous process of symbolic formulation—is passed over in virtual silence. Both interest theory and strain theory go directly from source analysis to consequence analysis without ever seriously examining ideologies as systems of interacting symbols, as patterns of interworking meanings. Themes are outlined, of course; among the content analysts, they are even counted. But they are referred for elucidation, not to other themes nor to any sort of semantic theory, but either backward to the affect they presumably mirror or forward to the social reality they presumably distort. The problem of how, after all, ideologies transform sentiment into significance and so make it socially available is short-circuited by the crude device of placing particular symbols and particular strains (or interests) side by side in such a way that the fact that the first are derivatives of the second seems mere common sense— or at least post-Freudian post-Marxian common sense. And so, if the analyst be deft enough, it does.[3] The connection is not thereby explained but merely educed. The nature of the relationship between the socio-psychological stresses that incite ideological attitudes and the elaborate symbolic structure through which those attitudes are given a public existence is much too complicated to be comprehended in terms of a vague and unexamined notion of emotive resonance.

It is of singular interest in this connection that, although the general stream of social scientific theory has been deeply influenced by almost every major intellectual movement of the last century and a half—Marxism, Darwinism, utilitarianism, idealism, Freudianism, behaviorism, positivism, operationalism—and has attempted to capitalize on virtually every important field of methodological innovation from ecology, ethology, and comparative psychology to game theory, cybernetics, and statistics, it has, with very few exceptions, been virtually untouched by one of the most important trends in recent thought: the effort to construct an independent science of what Kenneth Burke (1941) has called "symbolic action."[4] Neither the work of such philosophers as Peirce, Wittgenstein, Cassirer, Langer, Ryle, or Morris nor of such literary critics as Coleridge, Eliot, Burke, Empson, Blackmur, Brooks, or Auerbach seems to have had any appreciable impact on the general pattern of social scientific analysis.[5] Aside from a few more venturesome (and largely programmatic) linguists—a Whorf or a Sapir—the questions of how symbols symbolize, how they function to mediate meanings has simply been bypassed. "The embarrassing fact," the physician *cum* novelist Walker Percy has written, "is that there does not exist today—a natural empirical science of symbolic behavior *as such* . . . Sapir's gentle chiding about the lack of a science of symbolic behavior and the need of such a science is more conspicuously true today than it was thirty-five years ago" (Percy 1961).[6]

It is the absence of such a theory and in particular the absence of any analytical framework within which to deal with figurative language that have reduced sociologists to viewing ideologies as elaborate cries of pain. With no notion of how metaphor, analogy, irony, ambiguity, pun, paradox, hyperbole, rhythm, and all the other elements of what we lamely call "style" operate—even, in a majority of cases, with no recognition that these devices are of any importance in casting personal attitudes into public form, sociologists lack the symbolic resources out of which to construct a more incisive formulation. At the same time that the arts have been establishing the cognitive power of "distortion" and philosophy has been undermining the adequacy of an emotivist theory of meanings, social scientists have been rejecting the first and embracing the second. It is not therefore surprising that they evade the problem of construing the import of ideological assertions by simply failing to recognize it as a problem.[7]

In order to make explicit what I mean, let me take an example that is, I hope, so thoroughly trivial in itself as both to still any suspicions that I have a hidden concern with the substance of the political issue involved and, more important, to bring home the point that concepts developed for the analysis of the more elevated aspects of culture—poetry, for example—are applicable to the more lowly ones without in any way blurring the enormous qualitative distinctions between the two. In discussing the cognitive inadequacies by which ideology is defined for them, Sutton et al. use as an example of the ideologist's tendency to "oversimplify" the denomination by organized labor of the Taft-Hartley Act as a "slave labor law":

> Ideology tends to be simple and clear-cut, even where its simplicity and clarity do less than justice to the subject under discussion. The ideological picture uses sharp lines and contrasting blacks and whites. The ideologist exaggerates and caricatures in the fashion of the cartoonist. In contrast, a scientific description of social phenomena is likely to be fuzzy and indistinct. In recent labor ideology the Taft-Hartley Act has been a "slave labor act." By no dispassionate examination does the Act merit this label. Any detached assessment of the Act would have to consider its many provisions individually. On any set of values, even those of trade unions themselves, such an assessment would yield a mixed verdict. But mixed verdicts are not the stuff of ideology. They are too complicated, too fuzzy. Ideology must categorize the Act as a whole with a symbol to rally workers, voters and legislators to action. (1956:4-5)

Leaving aside the merely empirical question of whether or not it is in fact true that ideological formulations of a given set of social phenomena are inevitably "simpler" than scientific formulations of the same phenomena, there is in this argument a curiously depreciatory—one might even say "over simple"—view of the thought processes of labor-union leaders on the one hand and "workers, voters and legislators" on the other. It is rather hard to believe that either those who coined and disseminated the slogan themselves believed or expected anyone else to believe that the law would actually reduce (or was intended to reduce) the American worker to the status of a slave or that the segment of the public for whom the slogan had meaning perceived it in any such terms. Yet it is precisely this flattened view of other people's mentalities that leaves the sociologist with only two interpretations, both inadequate, of whatever effectiveness the symbol has: Either it deceives the uninformed (according to interest theory), or it excites the unreflective (according to strain theory). That it might in fact draw its power from its capacity to grasp, formulate, and communicate social realities that elude the tempered language of science, that it may mediate more complex meanings than its literal reading suggests, is not even considered. "Slave act" may be, after all, not a label but a trope.

More exactly, it appears to be a metaphor or at least an attempted metaphor. Although very few social scientists seem to have read much of it, the literature on metaphor—"the power whereby language, even with a small vocabulary manages to embrace a multi-million things"— is vast and by now in reasonable agreement.[8] In metaphor one has, of course, a stratification of meaning, in which an incongruity of sense on one level produces an influx of significance on another. As Percy has pointed out, the feature of metaphor that has most troubled philosophers (and, he might have added, scientists) is that it is "wrong": "It asserts of one thing that it is something else." And, worse yet, it tends to be most effective when most "wrong" (Percy 1958a). The power of a metaphor derives precisely from the interplay between the discordant meanings it symbolically coerces into a unitary conceptual framework and from the degree to which that coercion is successful in overcoming the psychic resistance such semantic tension inevitably generates in anyone in a position to perceive it. When it works, a metaphor transforms a false identification (for example, of the labor policies of the Republican Party and of those of the Bolsheviks) into an apt analogy; when it misfires, it is a mere extravagance.

That for most people the "slave labor law" figure was, in fact, pretty much a misfire (and therefore never served with any effectiveness as "a symbol to rally workers, voters and legislators to action") seems evident enough, and it is this failure, rather than its supposed clear-cut simplicity, that makes it seem no more than a cartoon. The semantic tension between the image of a conservative Congress outlawing the closed shop and of the prison camps of Siberia was—apparently —too great to be resolved into a single conception, at least by means of so rudimentary a stylistic device as the slogan. Except (perhaps) for a few enthusiasts, the analogy did not appear; the false identification remained false. But failure is not inevitable, even on such an elementary level. Although a most unmixed verdict, Sherman's "war is hell" is no social-science proposition. Even Sutton and his associates would probably not regard it as either an exaggeration or a caricature.

More important, however, than any assessment of the adequacy of the two tropes as such is the fact that, as the meanings they attempt to spark against one another are after all socially rooted, the success or failure of the attempt is relative not only to the power of the stylistic mechanisms employed but also to precisely those sorts of factor upon which strain theory concentrates its attention. The tensions of the Cold War, the fears of a labor movement only recently emerged from a bitter struggle for existence, and the threatened eclipse of New Deal liberalism after two decades of dominance set the sociopsychological stage both for the appearance of the "slave labor" figure and—when it proved unable to work them into a cogent analogy—for its miscarriage. The militarists of 1934 Japan who opened their pamphlet on *Basic Theory of National Defense and Suggestions for Its Strengthening* with the resounding familial metaphor, "War is the father of creation and the mother of culture," would no doubt have found Sherman's maxim as unconvincing as he would have found theirs.[9] They were energetically preparing for an imperialist war in an ancient nation seeking its footing in the modern world; he was wearily pursuing a civil war in an unrealized nation torn by domestic hatreds. It is thus not truth that varies with social, psychological, and cultural contexts but the symbols we construct in our unequally effective attempts to grasp it. War *is* hell and *not* the mother of culture, as the Japanese eventually discovered—although no doubt they express the fact in a grander idiom.

The sociology of knowledge ought to be called the sociology of meaning, for what is socially determined is not the nature of conception but the vehicles of conception. In a community that drinks its coffee black, Henle remarks, to praise a girl with "you're the cream in my coffee" would give entirely the wrong impression; and, if omnivorousness were regarded as a more significant characteristic of bears than their clumsy roughness, to call a man "an old bear" might mean not that he was crude but that he had catholic tastes (Henle 1958:4-5). Or, to take an example from Burke, since in Japan people smile on mentioning the death of a close friend, the semantic equivalent (behaviorally as well as verbally) in American English is not "he smiled" but "his face fell"; for, with such a rendering, we are "translating the accepted social usage of Japan into the corresponding accepted social usage of the West" (Burke 1957:149). And, closer to the ideological realm, Sapir has pointed out that the chairmanship of a committee has the figurative force we give it only because we hold that "administrative functions somehow stamp a person as superior to those who are being directed"; "should people come to feel that administrative functions are little more than symbolic automatisms, the chairmanship of a committee would be recognized as little more than a petrified symbol and the particular value that is now felt to inhere in it would tend to disappear" (Sapir 1949:568). The case is no different for "slave labor law." If forced labor camps come, for whatever reasons, to play a less prominent role in the American image of the Soviet Union, it will not be the symbol's veracity that has dissolved but its very meaning, its capacity to be *either* true or false. One must simply frame the argument—that the Taft-Hartley Act is a mortal threat to organized labor—in some other way.

In short, between an ideological figure like "slave labor act" and the social realities of American life in the midst of which it appears, there exists a subtlety of interplay, which concepts like "distortion," "selectivity," or "oversimplification" are simply incompetent to formulate.[10] Not only is the semantic structure of the figure a good deal more complex than it appears on the surface, but an analysis of that structure forces one into tracing a multiplicity of referential connections between it and social reality, so that the final picture is one of a configuration of dissimilar meanings out of whose interworking both the expressive power and the rhetorical force of the final symbol derive. This interworking is itself a social process, an occurrence not "in the head" but in that public world where "people talk together, name things, make assertions, and to a degree understand each other" (Percy 1961). The study of symbolic action is no less a sociological discipline than the study of small groups, bureaucracies, or the changing role of the American woman; it is only a good deal less developed.

Asking the question that most students of ideology fail to ask— what, precisely, do we mean when we assert that sociopsychological strains are "expressed" in symbolic forms?—gets one, therefore, very quickly into quite deep water indeed; into, in fact, a somewhat untraditional and apparently paradoxical theory of the nature of human thought as a public and not, or at least not fundamentally, a private activity (Ryle 1949). The details of such a theory cannot be pursued any distance here, nor can any significant amount of evidence be marshalled to support it. But at least its general outlines must be sketched if we are to find our way back from the elusive world of symbols and semantic process to the (apparently) solider one of sentiments and institutions, if we are to trace with some circumstantiality the modes of interpenetration of culture, personality, and social system.

The defining proposition of this sort of approach to thought *en plein air*—what, following Galanter and Gerstenhaber (1956), we may call "the extrinsic theory"—is that thought consists of the construction and manipulation of symbol systems, which are employed as models of other systems, physical, organic, social, psychological, and so forth, in such a way that the structure of these other systems—

and, in the favorable case, how they may therefore be expected to behave—is, as we say, "understood." Thinking, conceptualization, formulation, comprehension, understanding, or what-have-you consists not of ghostly happenings in the head but of a matching of the states and processes of symbolic models against the states and processes of the wider world:

> Imaginal thinking is neither more nor less than constructing an image of the environment, running the model faster than the environment, and predicting that the environment will behave as the model does. . . . The first step in the solution of a problem consists in the construction of a model or image of the "relevant features" of the [environment]. These models can be constructed from many things, including parts of the organic tissue of the body and, by man, paper and pencil or actual artifacts. Once a model has been constructed it can be manipulated under various hypothetical conditions and constraints. The organism is then able to "observe" the outcome of these manipulations, and to project them onto the environment so that prediction is possible. According to this view, an aeronautical engineer is thinking when he manipulates a model of a new airplane in a wind tunnel. The motorist is thinking when he runs his fingers over a line on a map, the finger serving as a model of the relevant aspects of the automobile, the map as a model of the road. External models of this kind are often used in thinking about complex [environments]. Images used in covert thinking depend upon the availability of the physico-chemical events of the organism which must be used to form models. (Galanter and Gerstenhaber, 1956:219)[11]

This view does not, of course, deny consciousness: It defines it. Every conscious perception is, as Percy has argued, an act of recognition, a pairing in which an object (or an event, an act, an emotion) is identified by placing it against the background of an appropriate symbol:

> It is not enough to say that one is conscious *of* something; one is also conscious of something being something. There is a difference between the apprehension of a gestalt (a chicken perceived the Jastrow effect as well as a human) and the grasping of it under its symbolic vehicle. As I gaze about the room, I am aware of a series of almost effortless acts of *matching*: seeing an object and knowing what it is. If my eye falls upon an unfamiliar something, I am immediately aware that one term of the match is missing, I ask what [the object] is—an exceedingly mysterious question. (Percy, 1958b:638)

What is missing and what is being asked for are an applicable symbolic model under which to subsume the "unfamiliar something" and so render it familiar:

> If I see an object at some distance and do not quite recognize it, I may see it, actually see it, as a succession of different things, each rejected by the criterion of fit as I come closer, until one is positively certified. A patch of sunlight in a field I may actually see as a rabbit—a seeing which goes much further than the guess that it may be a rabbit; no, the perceptual gestalt is so construed, actually stamped by the essence of rabbitness: I could have sworn it was a rabbit. On coming closer, the sunlight pattern changes enough so that

the rabbit-cast is disallowed. The rabbit vanishes and I make another cast: it is a paper bag, and so on. But most significant of all, even the last, the "correct" recognition is quite as mediate an apprehension as the incorrect ones; it is also a cast, a pairing, an approximation. And let us note in passing that even though it is correct, even though it is borne out by all indices, it may operate quite as effectively to conceal as to discover. When I recognize a strange bird as a sparrow, I tend to dispose of the bird under its appropriate formulation: it is only a sparrow. (Percy, 1958b:639)

Despite the somewhat intellectualist tone of these various examples, the extrinsic theory of thought is extendable to the affective side of human mentality as well (Langer 1953). As a road map transforms mere physical locations into "places," connected by numbered routes and separated by measured distances, and so enables us to find our way from where we are to where we want to go, so a poem like, for example, Hopkins's "Felix Randal" provides, through the evocative power of its charged language, a symbolic model of the emotional impact of premature death, which, if we are as impressed with its penetration as with the road map's, transforms physical sensations into sentiments and attitudes and enables us to react to such a tragedy not "blindly" but "intelligently." The central rituals of religion—a mass, a pilgrimage, a corroboree—are symbolic models (here more in the form of activities than of words) of a particular sense of the divine, a certain sort of devotional mood, which their continual re-enactment tends to produce in their participants. Of course, as most acts of what is usually called "cognition" are more on the level of identifying a rabbit than operating a wind tunnel, so most of what is usually called "expression" (the dichotomy is often overdrawn and almost universally misconstrued) is mediated more by models drawn from popular culture than from high art and formal religious ritual. But the point is that the development, maintenance, and dissolution of "moods," "attitudes," "sentiments," and so forth are no more "a ghostly process occurring in streams of consciousness we are debarred from visiting" than is the discrimination of objects, events, structures, processes, and so forth in our environment. Here, too, "we are describing the ways in which . . . people conduct parts of their predominantly public behavior" (Ryle 1949:51).

Whatever their other differences, both so-called cognitive and so-called expressive symbols or symbol-systems have, then, at least one thing in common: They are extrinsic sources of information in terms of which human life can be patterned—extrapersonal mechanisms for the perception, understanding, judgment, and manipulation of the world. Culture patterns—religious, philosophical, aesthetic, scientific, ideological—are "programs"; they provide a template or blueprint for the organization of social and psychological processes, much as genetic systems provide such a template for the organization of organic processes. . . .[12]

The reason such symbolic templates are necessary is that, as has been often remarked, human behavior is inherently extremely plastic. Not strictly but only very broadly controlled by genetic programs or models—intrinsic sources of information—such behavior must, if it it to have any effective form at all, be controlled to a significant extent by extrinsic ones. Birds learn how to fly without wind tunnels, and whatever reactions lower animals have to death are in great part innate, physiologically preformed.[13] The extreme generality, diffuseness, and variability of man's innate response capacities mean that the particular pattern his behavior takes is guided predominantly by cultural rather than genetic templates, the latter setting the overall psychophysical context within which precise activity sequences are organized by the former. The tool-making, laughing, or lying animal, man, is also the incomplete—or, more accurately, self-completing—animal. The agent of his own realization, he creates out of his general capacity for the construction of symbolic models the specific capabilities that define him. Or—to return at last to our subject—it is through the construction of ideologies, schematic images of social order, that man makes himself for better or worse a political animal.

Further, as the various sorts of cultural symbol-system are extrinsic sources of information, templates for the organization of social and psychological processes, they come most crucially into play in situations where the particular kind of information they contain is lacking, where institutionalized guides for behavior, thought, or feeling are weak or absent. It is in country unfamiliar emotionally or topographically that one needs poems and road maps.

So too with ideology. In polities firmly embedded in Edmund Burke's golden assemblage of "ancient opinions and rules of life," the role of ideology, in any explicit sense, is marginal. In such truly traditional political systems the participants act as (to use another Burkean phrase) men of untaught feelings; they are guided both emotionally and intellectually in their judgments and activities by unexamined prejudices, which do not leave them "hesitating in the moment of decision, sceptical, puzzled and unresolved." But when, as in the revolutionary France Burke was indicting and in fact in the shaken England from which, as perhaps his nation's greatest ideologue, he was indicting it, those hallowed opinions and rules of life come into question, the search for systematic ideological formulations, either to reinforce them or to replace them, flourishes. The function of ideology is to make an autonomous politics possible by providing the authoritative concepts that render it meaningful, the suasive images by means of which it can be sensibly grasped.[14]

It is, in fact, precisely at the point at which a political system begins to free itself from the immediate governance of received tradition, from the direct and detailed guidance of religious or philosophical canons on the one hand and from the unreflective precepts of conventional moralism on the other, that formal ideologies tend first to emerge and take hold.[15] The differentiation of an autonomous polity implies the differentiation, too, of a separate and distinct cultural model of political action, for the older, unspecialized models are either too comprehensive or too concrete to provide the sort of guidance such a political system demands. Either they trammel political behavior by encumbering it with transcendental significance, or they stifle political imagination by binding it to the blank realism of habitual judgment. It is when neither a society's most general cultural orientations nor its most down-to-earth, "pragmatic" ones suffice any longer to provide an adequate image of political process that ideologies begin to become crucial as sources of sociopolitical meanings and attitudes.

In one sense, this statement is but another way of saying that ideology is a response to strain. But now we are including *cultural* as well as social and psychological strain. It is a loss of orientation that most directly gives rise to ideological activity, an inability, for lack of usable models, to comprehend the universe of civic rights and responsibilities in which one finds oneself located. The development of a differentiated polity (or of greater internal differentiation within such a polity) may and commonly does bring with it severe social dislocation and psychological tension. But it also brings with it conceptual confusion, as the established images of political order fade into irrelevance or are driven into disrepute. The reason why the French Revolution was, at least up to its time, the greatest incubator of extremist ideologies, "progressive" and "reactionary" alike, in human history was not that either personal insecurity or social disequilibrium were deeper and more pervasive than at many earlier periods—though they were deep and pervasive enough—but because the central organizing principle of political life, the divine right of kings, was destroyed.[16] It is a confluence of sociopsychological strain and an absence of cultural resources by means of which to make (political, moral, or economic) sense of that strain, each exacerbating the other, that sets the stage for the rise of systematic (political, moral, economic) ideologies.

And it is, in turn, the attempt of ideologies to render otherwise incomprehensible social situations meaningful, to so construe them as to make it possible to act purposefully within them, that accounts both for the ideologies' highly figurative nature and for the intensity with which, once accepted, they are held. As metaphor extends language by broadening its semantic range, enabling it to express meanings it cannot or at least cannot yet express literally, so the head-on clash of literal meanings in ideology—the irony, the hyperbole, the overdrawn antithesis—provides novel symbolic frames against which to match the myriad "unfamiliar somethings" that, like a journey to a strange country, are produced by a transformation in political life. Whatever else ideologies may be—projections of unacknowledged fears, disguises for ulterior motives, phatic expressions of group solidarity—they are, most distinctively, maps of problematic social reality and matrices for the creation of collective conscience. Whether, in any particular case, the map is accurate or the conscience creditable is a separate question, to which one can hardly give the same answer for Nazism and Zionism, for the nationalisms of McCarthy and of Churchill, for the defenders of segregation and its opponents.

NOTES

*Excerpted from Clifford Geertz, "Ideology as a Cultural System," in David E. Apter, ed., *Ideology and Discontent* (New York: Free Press, 1964). Reprinted by permission of the publisher. Footnotes and referencing adapted.

[1]The quotations are from the most eminent recent interest theorist, C. Wright Mills (1958:54, 65).

[2]For the general schema, see Parsons (1951), especially chs. 1 and 7. The fullest development of the strain theory is in Sutton et al. (1956), especially ch. 15.

[3]Perhaps the most impressive tour de force in this paratactic genre is Nathan Leites's *A Study of Bolshevism* (1953).

[4]In the following discussion, I use *symbol* broadly in the sense of any physical, social, or cultural act or object that serves as the vehicle for a conception. For an explication of this view, under which fire and the Cross are equally symbols, see S. Langer (1960), pp. 60-66.

[5]Useful general summaries of the tradition of literary criticism can be found in Hyman (1948), and in Wellek and Warren (1958). A similar summary of the somewhat more diverse philosophical development is apparently not available, but the seminal works are Peirce (1931-1958), Cassirer (1923-1929), Morris (1944), and Wittgenstein (1953).

[6]The reference is to Sapir's "The Status of Linguistics as a Science," originally published in 1929 (Sapir 1949).

[7]A partial exception to this stricture, although marred by his obsession with power as the sum and substance of politics, is Lasswell's "Style in the Language of Politics" (Lasswell et al. 1949:20-39). It also should be remarked that the emphasis on verbal symbolism in the following discussion is merely for the sake of simplicity and is not intended to deny the importance of plastic, theatrical, or other nonlinguistic devices—the rhetoric of uniforms, floodlit stages, and marching bands—in ideological thought.

[8]An excellent recent review is to be found in Henle (1958:173-195). The quotation is from Langer (1960:117).

[9]Quoted in Crowley (1958).

[10]Metaphor is, of course, not the only stylistic resource upon which ideology draws. Metonymy ("All I have to offer is blood, sweat and tears"), hyperbole ("The thousand-year Reich"), meiosis ("I shall return"), synechdoche ("Wall Street"), oxymoron ("Iron Curtain"), personification ("The hand that held the dagger has plunged it into the back of its neighbor"), and all the other figures the classical rhetoricians so painstakingly collected and so carefully classified are utilized over and over again, as are such syntactical devices as antithesis, inversion, and repetition; such prosodic ones as rhyme, rhythm, and alliteration; such literary ones as irony, eulogy, and sarcasm. Nor is all ideological expression figurative. The bulk of it consists of quite literal, not to say flat-footed, assertions, which, a certain tendency toward *prima facie* implausibility aside, are difficult to distinguish from properly scientific statements: "The history of all hitherto existing society is the history of class struggles"; "the whole of the morality of Europe is based upon the values which are useful to the herd"; and so forth. As a cultural system, an ideology that has developed beyond the stage of mere sloganeering consists of an intricate structure of interrelated meanings—interrelated in terms of the semantic mechanisms that formulate them—of which the two-level organization of an isolated metaphor is but a feeble representation.

[11]I have quoted this incisive passage before, in a paper attempting to set the extrinsic theory of thought in the context of recent evolutionary, neurological, and cultural anthropological findings. See Geertz (1962).

[12]Compare: "In order to account for this selectivity, it is necessary to assume that the structure of the enzyme is related in some way to the structure of the gene. By a logical extension of this idea we arrive at the concept that the gene is a representation—blueprint so to speak—of the enzyme molecule, and that the function of the gene is to serve as a source of information regarding the structure of the enzyme. It seems evident that the synthesis of an enzyme—a giant protein molecule consisting of hundreds of amino acid units arranged end-to-end in a specific and unique order—requires a model or set of instructions of some kind. These instructions must be characteristic of the species; they must be automatically transmitted from generation to generation, and they must be constant yet capable of evolutionary change. The only known entity that could perform such a function is the gene. There are many reasons for believing that it transmits information, by acting as a model or template" (Horowitz 1956:85). See also Parsons 1959a.

[13]This point is perhaps somewhat too baldly put in light of recent analyses of animal learning; but the essential thesis—that there is a general trend toward a more diffuse, less determinate control of behavior by intrinsic (innate) parameters as one moves from lower to higher animals—seems well established. See Geertz (1962) where the whole argument, here strenuously compressed, is developed in full.

[14]Of course, there are moral, economic, and even aesthetic ideologies, as well as specifically political ones, but as very few ideologies of any social prominence lack political implications, it is perhaps permissible to view the problem here in this somewhat narrowed focus. In any case, the arguments developed for political ideologies apply with equal force to nonpolitical ones. For an analysis of a moral ideology cast in terms very similar to those developed in this paper, see Green (1961).

[15]That such ideologies may call, as did Burke's or De Maistre's, for the reinvigoration of custom or the reimposition of religious hegemony is, of course, no contradiction. One constructs arguments for tradition only when its credentials have been questioned. To the degree that such appeals are successful they bring.

not a return to naive traditionalism, but ideological retraditionalization—an altogether different matter. See Mannheim (1953), especially pp. 94-98.

[16]It is important to remember, too, that the principle was destroyed long before the king; it was to the successor principle that he was, in fact, a ritual sacrifice: "When [Saint-Just] exclaims: 'To determine the principle in virtue of which the accused [Louis XVI] is perhaps to die, is to determine the principle by which the society that judges him lives,' he demonstrates that it is the philosophers who are going to kill the King: the King must die in the name of the social contract" (Camus, 1958:114).

REFERENCES

Burke, Kenneth, 1941. *The Philosophy of Literary Form, Studies in Symbolic Action* (Baton Rouge: Louisiana State University Press).
_____, 1957. *Counter-statement* (Chicago: University of Chicago Press).
Camus, Albert, 1958. *The Rebel* (New York: Knopf).
Cassirer, Ernst, 1923-1929. *Die Philosophie der symbolischen Formen*, 3 vols. (Berlin: B. Cassirer).
Crowley, James, 1958. Japanese Army Factionalism in the Early 1930's. *The Journal of Asian Studies* 21:309-326.
Galanter, Eugene, and Murray Gerstenhaber, 1956. On Thought: The Extrinsic Theory. *Psychological Review* 63:218-227.
Geertz, Clifford, 1962. The Growth of Culture and the Evolution of Mind. In *Theories of the Mind*, J. Scher, ed. (New York: Free Press), pp. 713-740.
Green, Arnold L., 1961. The Ideology of Anti-Fluoridation Leaders. *The Journal of Social Issues* 17:13-25.
Henle, Paul, ed., 1958. *Language, Thought and Culture* (Ann Arbor: University of Michigan Press).
Horowitz, N. H., 1956. The Gene. *Scientific American* 195:34, 78-86.
Hyman, Stanley Edgar, 1948. *The Armed Vision* (New York: Knopf).
Langer, Suzanne, 1953. *Feeling and Form* (New York: Scribners).
_____, 1960. *Philosophy in a New Key*, 4th ed. (Cambridge: Harvard University Press).
Lasswell, Harold D., N. Leites, and Associates, 1949. *Language of Politics* (New York: G. W. Stewart).
Leites, Nathan, 1953. *A Study of Bolshevism* (New York: Free Press).
Mannheim, Karl, 1953. Conservative Thought. In *Essays on Sociology and Social Psychology by Karl Mannheim* (New York: Oxford University Press), pp. 74-164.
Mills, C. Wright, 1958. *The Causes of World War Three* (New York: Simon and Schuster).
Morris, Charles W., 1944. *Signs, Language and Behavior* (Englewood Cliffs: Prentice-Hall).
Parsons, Talcott, 1951. *The Social System* (New York: Free Press).
_____, 1959a. An Approach to Psychological Theory in Terms of the Theory of Action. In *Psychology: A Study of a Science*, S. Koch, ed., vol. 3 (New York: McGraw Hill), pp. 612-711.
_____, 1959b. An Approach to the Sociology of Knowledge. In *Transactions of the Fourth World Congress of Sociology, Milan and Stressa* (Bari: Laterza), pp. 24-49.
Peirce, Charles S., 1931-1958. *Collected Papers*, C. Hartshorne and P. Weiss, eds., 8 vols. (Cambridge: Harvard University Press).
Percy, Walker, 1958a. Metaphor as Mistake. *The Sewanee Review* 66:79-99.
_____, 1958b. Symbol, Consciousnes and Intersubjectivity. *Journal of Philosophy* 55:631-641.

_____, 1961. The Symbolic Structure of Interpersonal Process. *Psychiatry* 24:39-52.

Ryle, Gilbert, 1949. *The Concept of Mind* (New York: Hutchinson's University Library).

Sapir, Edward, 1949. *Selected Writings of Edward Sapir,* D. Mandelbaum, ed. (Berkeley: University of California Press).

Sutton, Francis X., Seymore E. Harris, Carl Kaysen, and James Tobin, 1956. *The American Business Creed* (Cambridge: Harvard University Press).

Wellek, Rene, and Austin Warren, 1958. *Theory of Literature,* 2nd ed. (New York: Harcourt Brace).

White, Winston, 1961. *Beyond Conformity* (New York: Free Press).

Wittgenstein, Ludwig, 1953. *Philosophical Investigations* (Oxford: B. Blackwell).

The Prophecy and the Law: Symbolism and Social Action in Seventh-day Adventism

Frank E. Manning

In his definitional essay "Religion as a Cultural System," Geertz proposed the following thesis: "Sacred symbols function to synthesize a people's ethos—the tone, character, and quality of their life, its moral and aesthetic style and mood—and their world-view—the picture they have of the way things in sheer actuality are, their most comprehensive ideas of order" (1966:3). A decade after that essay's appearance, however, we have little precise understanding of the way in which symbols work to establish dialectical interplay and perceived consistency between the cognitive and ethical spheres of religion. In this paper I would like to work toward such an understanding with reference to Seventh-day Adventism. Field research was conducted in the anglophonic West Indies, primarily Barbados, where Adventism is the fastest growing reform movement in Christianity. I will first explicate the conceptual meanings embodied in Adventism's dominant symbols and consider how these meanings bear on ethical demands. I will then compare Adventism to Reformation Protestantism as analyzed by Weber (1958) and discuss the significance of this comparison in terms of development and modernization in new nations.

The unique belief system[1] of Seventh-day Adventism is condensed in two dominant symbols: the sanctuary and the Sabbath. The sanctuary is the focal point of a complex interpretation of history and cosmos. The Sabbath represents law and its crucial significance in the man-to-God relationship. These two symbols are the distinguishing marks of a third dominant symbol which relates belief to social identity: the remnant church. An exegetical discussion of the sanctuary, the Sabbath, and the remnant church is thus an initiation (academically at least) into the Adventist metaphysic.

The sanctuary symbol takes its most important meaning from an apocalyptical vision in the book of Daniel. After the prophet has seen a series of beasts assume control over the earth, he hears one angel ask another how long the sanctuary will be trodden under foot. It is answered, "Unto two thousand and three hundred days; then shall the sanctuary be cleansed" (Daniel 8:14).[2]

From the following chapter of Daniel the deduction is made that this period began in 457 B.C.—the date when Artaxerxes restored civil government to the Jewish nation. As a prophetic day is believed equivalent to a literal year (Numbers 14:34; Ezekiel 4:6), the period ended in 1844. The nineteenth-century Millerite movement developed this calculation and concluded that the cleansing of the sanctuary meant the end of the world. When their prediction failed to materialize the movement's enthusiasm soon evaporated (Wilson 1970:99).

Some of the Millerites, however, clung to the significance of 1844 but developed a new understanding of the sanctuary. Among them was the group which was later to organize formally as Seventh-day Adventists. Moved by the insight of one of their members, they determined that the cleansing of the sanctuary was a cosmic analogue of the Day of Atonement in the Old Testament ritual system. Once a year the Jewish high priest entered the Holy of Holies, the second room of the sanctuary. There he cleansed the sanctuary with the sacrificial blood of a goat representing the Lord, thus atoning for the sins of the people. These sins were then transferred to a second goat (the scapegoat) representing Satan, which was banished into the wilderness. Similarly, since 1844 Christ has been in the second room of the heavenly sanctuary, cleansing it and atoning for sins by applying the redemptive merits of his own sacrifice on earth. This process consists of conducting an investigative judgment of all mankind and pleading before God the Father on behalf of those deemed worthy. When this work is finished, the sins of repentant humanity will be finally blotted out and placed on Satan; Christ will come to earth in his second advent, ending the present world order and ushering in the millenium.

The sanctuary prophecy is understood in connection with a number of other prophecies found in Hebrew and Christian apocalyptical writings. One of these is the seventy weeks allotted to the Jewish people (Daniel 9:24-27). The angel Gabriel divides the first sixty-nine weeks of this prophecy into a seven-week period during which Jerusalem will be rebuilt and a sixty-two-week period after which the Messiah will come. The Messiah will confirm the covenant during the seventieth week, but will be "cut off" in the midst of it. Adventists see the seven-week or forty-nine-year period of this prophecy as having occurred between 457 B.C., when Ezra was given the decree to restore Jerusalem (Ezra 7:7, 12-13), and 408 B.C., when the restoration was completed. The next sixty-two weeks or 434 years reached to A.D. 27, the year, Adventists claim, when Christ was baptized and thus assumed the role of Messiah. Christ conducted his earthly ministry during the seventieth week, but in the midst of it—three and a half years after his baptism—he was crucified. After another three and a half years Stephen was stoned, thus ending the period assigned to the Jews as the chosen people. The correlation of these seventy weeks or 490 years to historical events strengthens the belief that Christ has been cleansing the heavenly sanctuary since 1844, as the seventy weeks are taken as the first part of the twenty-three hundred days.

Another prophecy carefully studied by Adventists is that of the four great kingdoms portrayed in the second, seventh, and eighth chapters of Daniel. The first three kingdoms are scripturally identified as Babylon, Media-Persia, and Greece. The fourth and most horrendous is seen as Rome. The prophecy further claims that out of this fourth kingdom there will arise another power that will repress the saints of God and "think to change times and laws" (Daniel 7:25). To Adventists, this final and most evil of all regimes is the papacy. It attempted to change times and laws by moving the Sabbath from the seventh day of the week to the first and by rearranging the decalogue to eliminate the second commandment and expand the tenth commandment into two separate precepts.

The papacy, however, was not meant to reign unchallenged forever. It was given "a time, and times, and dividing of time" (Daniel 7:25) as its period of rule. As Adventists believe that a "time" denoted a Hebrew year or 360 days, they interpret this period as three and a half years or 1,260 days—a calculation that is corroborated in the book of Revelation, where there is explicit mention of 1,260 days being allotted to a dragon to dominate the earth while a celestial woman representing the true church of Christ is forced into the wilderness (Revelation 12:1-14). In literal time this means that the papacy was given 1,260 years of unchallenged rule. Adventists see this period as having begun between 533, when Justinian recognized the pope as "head of all the churches," and 538, when the papacy vanquished its Arian opposition, and as having ended between 1793, when the French Revolution suppressed Roman Catholicism under the Reign of Terror and 1798, when the French army entered Rome and imprisoned the pope.

The decline of the papacy after 1798 was not a final demise; it was further prophesied that the beast would recover from its deadly wound and receive the acclamation of the world (Revelation 13:3). Still, the weakening of the papacy was a prelude to the "time of the end" (Daniel 12:9), the period when men would begin to understand prophetic truths hitherto sealed in the scriptures. This period is also marked by three angelic messages conveying God's last statement to the world in preparation for His second coming. The first angel proclaims that the hour of judgment is at hand (Revelation 14:6-7); this is seen as an announcement of Christ's passage into the second room of the heavenly sanctuary in 1844. The second angel heralds that Babylon is fallen (Revelation 14:8); this is seen as a statement that evil and error have been exposed. The third angel proclaims the appearance of those who "keep the commandments of God" and the "faith of Jesus" (Revelation 14:9-12). Adventists interpret this message as a reference to themselves. Only a handful of the hundreds of Christian denominations keep the entire ten commandments, the rest having followed the papacy in violating the Sabbath precept by hallowing the first day of the week instead of the seventh. And no other church has the faith or testimony of Jesus, defined as the "spirit of prophecy" (Revelation 19:10) and believed by Adventists to have been manifest especially in Ellen White, whose voluminous writings have governed the church since its formal organization in the 1860's. As the distinctive Sabbath-keeping church of prophecy, Adventists conclude that they are the "remnant" predicted to surface at the end of the papacy's period of monolithic rule (Revelation 12:17). Identification with the remnant symbol gives them an ancestry and a destiny transcending the short compass of their actual history. Their ancestry makes them the spiritual heirs of the obscure sects that allegedly remained faithful to Christian commands during the long centuries of Satanic persecution carried out through the agency of the papacy. Their destiny calls them to end this conflict against Satan by bringing truth to the world in the closing days of time.

As the commandment whose observance distinguishes Adventists from nearly all other Christian bodies, the Sabbath precept has taken on immense significance. Part of its broad meaning is communicated through what Turner (1967:54) calls the principle of *pars pro toto;* Sabbath-keeping is not merely one part of the law, but represents the law as a whole. This view is developed in a story that has been widely published in Adventist pamphlets, periodicals, and broadcasts. The scenario is the home of a professed infidel who has invited an Adventist minister to dinner. After the meal the minister is verbally assaulted by the infidel, who contends that the law is a poorly conceived statement designed to intimidate ignorant people. The minister replies that the law is so perfectly coherent that a violation of one of its commands implies a violation of the entire law. He begins by citing the fourth commandment which requires keeping holy the Sabbath, a day that is

God's, not man's. To take the Sabbath for one's own usage is therefore stealing, a violation of the eighth commandment. It also implies a prior covetousness of the thing stolen, forbidden by the tenth commandment.

At this point the infidel is taken aback, but the minister continues to prosecute his elegant apology. He shows his adversary that by breaking the Sabbath the sinner has also done the following: he has put himself above God, a violation of the first commandment which says that God must be above all; he has made an idol of himself, a breach of the second commandment which forbids the making of idols; he has, in breaking the only commandment to which God's name is attached, violated the third commandment which prohibits taking God's name in vain; he has implicitly lied about the day set aside for worship and rest, and thereby broken the ninth commandment which forbids lying; he has disobeyed his creator, who is a heavenly father, thus violating the fifth commandment which requires one to honor his parents.

This relentless casuistry leaves the infidel thoroughly confused, but the minister feels compelled to finish the argument. The Sabbath breaker is a sinner, and since "the wages of sin is death" (Romans 6:23), he has transgressed the sixth commandment which forbids the taking of life. Finally, since God is scripturally likened to a husband and the sinner to an unchaste wife, the Sabbath breaker has violated the seventh commandment by committing a form of spiritual adultery. Thus through the nonobservance of the Sabbath the hapless sinner has broached the entire decalogue—an indication, in the words of the minister, that the fourth commandment is at the "very heart" of the law, deserving to be called the "greatest of all the commandments."

The Sabbath, then, has both a social structural referent as a mark of the remnant church and a logical referent as the center of the law as a whole. In this latter hermeneutic the Sabbath works to establish and sustain the fundamental importance of law in Adventist thought. Forensic images constitute some of the primary metaphors through which Adventists envision the divine trinity and its operations. The most familiar of these images is that conveyed by the sanctuary prophecy, that Christ has been conducting an investigative judgment in heaven since 1844. Alternately, Christ is viewed as a court advocate presenting cases to God the Father, a being whose very essence is revealed by law—in Adventist phrasing, law is a "transcript of the character of God" (*Questions on Doctrine* 1957:122). Similarly, the Holy Ghost is often understood as a solicitor or chamber advocate who resides in men during their life on earth, assisting them to eliminate sin from their lives.

The law is also the standard of righteousness. Adventists continually cite such New Testament passages as "If you love me, keep my commandments" (John 14:15) to show that Christ never intended to abrogate the law. The decalogue is the most basic expression of the law, but Adventists recognize the continuing validity of other precepts laid down in the Old Testament such as the complex Levitical dietary code. They dismiss as inapplicable only those precepts that are deemed "ceremonial," that is, those viewed as "types" which met their antitype in Christ and were therefore abolished or "nailed to the cross." Thus although faith and grace are the means of salvation, as throughout the Arminian Protestant tradition, law is the most symbolically elaborated aspect of man's relationship to God as well as the metaphorical denominator of man's understanding of God's nature and work.

Another line of meaning symbolized by the Sabbath pertains directly to the final events of history and hence to the events represented by the sanctuary and remnant church prophecies. Adventists believe that immediately before the second coming of Christ there will arise a coalition of world powers that will seek to make the observance of Sunday binding on all men. Those who succumb to this pressure will receive the "mark of the beast" (Revelations 13:16, 17) and the hideous punishment which it entails (Revelations 14:9-11). Those who maintain their allegiance to the seventh-day Sabbath will be numbered among the remnant destined for eternal reward when the heavenly sanctuary is finally cleansed of the stain of sin.

In closing this account of Adventist belief it should be stressed that I have given no more than a skeletal outline of an intricate and profound system. By focusing on the system's dominant symbols, however, it is possible to gain an acquaintance with those elements of belief that are the most recurrent and deeply meaningful. This leads to the problem posed at the outset of this paper. How do the symbols which formulate a worldview bear on the motivations that govern an ethos? How do Adventists respond to their understanding of prophecy and law and to their social identity as a remnant people?

Prophecy works to intellectualize and systematize ethical demands. This influence can be seen in the following account of conversion given by a young man in Barbados:

It [becoming an Adventist] wasn't a rash decision or a rash change. It was a gradual process of becoming convinced of the truth of the doctrine. You might say that a Christian will know when he's converted because of the change in his actions or the change in his life but, as I said, as you get to know more and more you begin to change more and more. It's a growing process as such. It's like a child, born and growing into maturity, into manhood. Each step of the way you become more and more acquainted with the doctrine and you become more and more Christian. There's no definite point of conversion.

Adventists often describe the gradual process of conversion as "accepting the message"—an in-group idiom referring to the apocalyptical message which announces the appearance of a commandment-keeping church of prophecy. Many of my informants maintained that they "read themselves into the message." Others recalled polemic exchanges which convinced them that the Adventist position was logically unassailable. One notable technique that led Barbadians into Adventism was the posting of sizable cash rewards by Adventist ministers or laymen for anyone who could prove that Saturday was not the Sabbath; as these rewards were never won, persons realized that the Adventist claim could resist any challenge.

Throughout an Adventist's life, education continues as the companion of edification and moral growth. All Adventists are members of the Sabbath school as well as the church. They study daily lessons centered on the Bible and Adventist writings and review the lessons on Saturday in classroom sessions organized into a half-dozen divisions from "cradle roll" to adult. Intellectual imagery pervades Adventist worship services. Ministers usually begin their sermons by stating that they are going to "study" with their congregations. Many come to church with briefcases in which they carry a Bible, lesson book, and materials for taking notes.

The intellectualism of the Adventist ethic is further evidenced by the frequent reference to persons who have sinned as "apostates" rather than the term more familiar in evangelical Protestantism, "backsliders." Church members, who, for example, have broken the Sabbath or committed fornication (the most common offenses in Barbados against Adventist morality) are categorized as having apostatized, an image suggesting forswearance of doctrine, rather than as having backslid, an image suggesting loss of self-control. This implies a kind of Lévi-Straussian understanding of the primacy of intellect over other aspects of consciousness; morality is rooted more in logic than in volition.

The influence of law on the Adventist ethic is complementary to that of prophecy. While the study of prophecy is the basis of moral regeneration, the keeping of law is the evidence of it. In their recently expanded efforts to absolve themselves of the charge of legalism made by revivalist groups, Adventists have emphasized that the law is not a means to salvation but a sign of it. In the words of the president of the Caribbean Union of Seventh-day Adventists, "We do not keep the ten commandments to be saved. We keep them because we are saved, and a saved man shows his salvation in Christ by obeying all that God tells him to do through God's enabling grace" (Thompson 1973:20). My informants often likened the law to a looking glass; it is an external, objective standard that enables one to perceive his inner spiritual condition.

Obedience to law, like study of prophecy, is an unrelenting ethical requirement. Adventists understand salvation in three dimensions: past, present, and future. The past dimension, justification, is forgiveness from previous sin. The present dimension, sanctification, is the life-long process of adhering to the divine mandate by steadfastly observing legal rule. To quote again from the Caribbean Union president, "When a man is justified and has been saved from the guilt of sin, then in the process of sanctification he brings his life into conformity to the will of God" (Thompson 1973:20). Continuous fidelity to the law prepares one for future salvation, to be realized after the second advent and millenium when Christ establishes His everlasting kingdom on earth for His obedient followers.

The asceticism of Adventist law requires the complete avoidance of "fetes" (dances, parties, shows, etc.) as well as the neighborhood "rum shop," the center of male sociability in Barbados. Abstention from such pleasures saves Adventists both time and money, which they subsequently invest in education and job training—courses of action which reinforce ascetic norms by encouraging deferment of gratification while one prepares for a long-term goal. Narratives such as the following are typical:

When I was in primary school my lone goal was to gain acceptance into secondary school. When I was in secondary school, I had varying ambitions: I wanted to be a doctor; I wanted to be a teacher; and later, when I got into fifth form, I wanted to be a businessman. Of course, my main objective was to sit my G.C.E. [General Certificate of Education] exams and pass them. Then when I finished secondary school I wanted to go to college.

One of the major goals of education and training is to qualify for a job that allows the observance of the Sabbath. In a society where the five-day work week did not gain acceptance in industry until the 1970's, this requirement has concentrated Adventists in a small number of occupations. A startling 44 percent of respondents in a survey I conducted[3] were teachers or church workers; of these, more than three-fourths were teachers, including those teaching in church schools. Another 14 percent of the respondents were self-employed, chiefly in commerce and agriculture. The adult children of respondents tended to follow these same occupations as well as another requiring more education, namely, medicine. Medical work does not cease on Saturday, but carries a dispensation from the Sabbath precept as it is viewed by Adventists as an act of mercy.

Besides fostering a sustained, methodical, life-long commitment to ethical action, the symbols of prophecy and law exert a rationalizing influence on the Adventist ethos. Both doctrine and precept are valued for their empirical validity and utility. The systematic correlation of prophetic archetypes and allegories with actual historical events is an example of such rationalization, as is the justification of law on pragmatic grounds. In discussing their abstinence from pork, for instance, my informants invariably stressed that the pig is a scavenger and therefore unclean, rather than that the pig is forbidden by Biblical taboo because it does not chew its cud (Leviticus 11:7).

The sustained, methodical asceticism and deliberate rationality of the Adventist ethic invites comparison with the ethic of early Calvinism. According to Weber (1958) the Calvinist envisioned himself in a direct but distant and unmediated relationship to God. God had assigned to each man a basic ethical imperative: to pursue his life's task, or calling, with austere rationalism and single-minded diligence. God in His inscrutable manner had also predestined some men to be saved and others to be damned in a life to come, but neither church membership nor ritual performance was of any use in indicating whether or not one was counted among God's elect.

The Calvinist's ethical response to this tormenting worldview derived from the conclusion that the best way to achieve conviction of salvation was to behave as if one were saved. Relentless labor for the glory of God and the betterment of man thus became the Calvinist's only reliable sign of righteousness. Every thought and action was to be systematically integrated into a total plan of work. Idleness and sensual indulgence were distractions from work and hence condemned. Magical shortcuts to salvation were irrational and thus reprehensible. Such convictions drove the Calvinist to organize his entire life into a continuous, methodical commitment to his God-given calling.

The calling, then, was the major symbol in Calvinism. It synthesized worldview and ethos, imparting meaning and value to life on earth. It gave work in the world what Weber called a "positive ethical sanction" (1958:74), making it the very essence of moral conduct. The results of the symbolic transformation of worldly work into a religious imperative were seen in the vast economic, political, legal, and scientific developments that modernized Western society.

In Adventism the symbols of prophecy and law parallel the Calvinist's calling. Although Adventists achieve salvation "by grace, through faith" (Ephesians 2:8), prophecy and law are the visible, external symbols of righteousness. Adherence to the ethical demands derived from these symbols requires Adventists to systematize and rationalize their entire lives in accordance with objective criteria. In this sense they closely parallel the Calvinist model.

Yet in their broader implications for social action, prophecy and law differ from the Calvinist calling. The fulfillment of a calling involved one directly in worldly activity. But when religious attention is focused on dogma and rule, one has, as Bellah (1965:82) notes, turned partially away from the world. Like sacramental systems and mystical exercises, prophecy and law offer a mediated form of salvation. The inspired ethical commitment to the continuous, rational pursuit of a calling among Weber's idealized Calvinists is thus replaced in Adventism by an inspired commitment to continuous, rational study of prophecy and obedience to law.

The mediating role of prophecy and law points to the church, the third dominant symbol in Adventism. Recognized by its possession of prophecy and its allegiance to law, the church has the converse task (left to the individual in classical and revivalist Protestantism) of interpreting prophecy and law, that is, of defining doctrine and pronouncing precept. The vital importance of the church is seen in the fact that its mission and program are represented by Adventists as the "Work." Those who do the Work on a full-time basis are the "Workers" and enjoy the highest recognition in the Adventist social system—an attraction that helps to explain why 18 percent of my survey respondents were church employees.

Here lies perhaps the most crucial difference between the Adventist and Calvinist ethics. In Calvinism "the whole world was a monastery and every man a monk." All worldly tasks were a morally meaningful calling. But in Adventism the term *calling* is used in the restricted sense of a religious vocation—a calling to the Work. Other occupations are acceptable, but only the Work is a moral imperative.

The partial fit of the Adventist ethic into the Calvinist ideal type has practical as well as theoretical relevance. The Weberian thesis that Calvinism and some of its classical theological descendants fostered the rise of a trained bourgeoisie who spurred the modernization of Western society in the seventeenth and eighteenth centuries raises the question of whether a similar religious movement can have a similar role today in societies struggling to develop. In short, can Adventism wield a modernizing influence in the Caribbean?

The socioeconomic profile of Barbadian Adventists is consonant with the Weberian argument that systematic, rational asceticism promotes social advancement. In my survey 54 percent of respondents were secondary school graduates, as compared to only 15 percent of the male working population of Barbados (1970 census). Similarly, three-quarters of my respondents were either self-employed or held professional or white collar positions whereas 55 percent of Barbadian men are found in production work, unskilled labor, or service jobs (1970 census). Among my married survey respondents only one-quarter lived in government housing or wooden chattel houses; the remaining three-quarters lived in stone bungalows, one of the primary indicators of middle class standing in West Indian society (Smith 1961:260).

Intergenerational upward mobility among Adventists is impressive. The eighteen respondents who were raised in Adventist homes or who became Advenists before age fifteen all held either professional or white collar positions or were self-employed; specifically, this sub-sample consisted of 45 percent professionals, 33 percent white collar workers, and 22 percent self-employed. Among the fathers of this same group there were only 5 percent professionals and 28 percent self-employed; 45 percent of the fathers were tradesmen, the same percentage of the respondents who were professionals.

An equally impressive pattern of mobility appears in the subsequent generation. In my survey there were thirteen men whose oldest son was over twenty-one years of age. All of these oldest sons were secondary school graduates, and more than half university graduates. By comparison, among their informant fathers there were 38 percent secondary graduates and no university graduates. In terms of occupations 61 percent of the sons were professionals and 23 percent held white collar positions, as compared to the fathers among whom there were 23 percent professionals and 23 percent white collar workers.

These few statistics indicate the broad outlines of a pattern. Adventists are recruited primarily from the lower and lower-middle classes. Within a generation they have usually achieved the criteria of middle-class standing in Barbadian society: completed secondary school education, a job outside of manual labor, and residence in a stone bungalow. Within two generations a majority have acquired university degrees and secured professional positions, thus breaking through into what might be termed an upper-middle class.

The respectable climb of Adventists into the ranks of an educated bourgeoisie is of significance in Barbados and other class-conscious new nations that have emerged from the breakup of the British colonial empire in the Caribbean. Adventists are becoming part of what is often called the "new elite"—the professional, managerial, and upper-echelon civil servant class which has gradually taken over the cultural authority and social privilege formerly held by the old elite of whites, mulattoes, and colonial officials.

Yet the personal success and mobility of Adventists has seemingly had less meaning to them than their special mission on earth—the Work. A striking example of the Work's moral resonance vis-à-vis secular activity is provided by a Barbadian Adventist entrepreneur whose approach to his business was strikingly similar to that of Weber's Calvinist-capitalists. He worked twelve hours a day six days a week, lived frugally, reinvested almost all of his profits, expanded his business every year, valued employees for efficiency more than friendship or kinship, organized a bureaucratic system of management, and even cited the Biblical proverb quoted by Benjamin Franklin: "Seest thou a man diligent in his business? he shall stand before kings" (Weber 1958:53). Yet while he found his business a challenge and a source of satisfaction, he said he probably would have gained a greater sense of fulfillment if he had become a Worker. He noted: "It's true that the church teaches that any honest job has dignity; but they also make it clear that anything outside the Work is inferior to it." He displayed a mild-mannered resentment of the ecclesiastical attitude, but had accommodated to it by becoming involved in such part-time yet demanding duties as holding evangelistic crusades and serving as lay elder. Moreover, he sent his two sons to Adventist schools for all their education. The older son was a teacher in an Adventist college; the younger son was still a student, but my informant said he hoped he too would enter the Work, even though it would mean that the business could not be passed down in the family. Might this example be closer to the pre-Calvinist merchant described by Peacock (1969: 49) for whom religion cured the guilt that work caused, than to the Calvinist entrepreneur for whom work cured the guilt that religion caused?

It is through the Work, in any event, that Adventists have made their most dynamic impact on the Caribbean as well as the impact most likely to change the social order rather than merely rearrange elite groups. While all of the Work has proselytization as its primary aim, social reform in such areas as medicine, education, welfare, and youth programs is closely integrated with missionary objectives. The medical "ministry," known as the "right arm of the church" (Herndon 1960:87) exemplifies the rationality with which reform is carried out. Like many revivalist groups, Adventists are greatly concerned about health. But whereas the revivalist response has been expressed chiefly in faith healing spectacles and curative rituals (cf. Hill 1973:849-853; Keber 1971:4-15), Adventsts have developed a multifaceted program that emphasizes nutrition, hygiene, and prevention as well as curing. The program includes the regular publication of a number of health journals, the manufacture and retail of health foods, organized periodic campaigns against health hazards such as drug abuse, and a world-wide network of hospitals, nursing homes, clinics, infirmaries, dispensaries, and schools for training doctors, nurses, and public health professionals. In the anglophonic Caribbean the church runs three hospitals, two dental clinics, three nursing homes, and a number of small medical and geriatric services. These facilities are generally regarded as superior to those provided by the region's national governments, as seen in the high rate (90 percent and over) of non-Adventist patients.

Comparable accomplishments have been made in other target areas of social reform. The church has the largest denominational school system in the anglophonic Caribbean, including two colleges,[4] about two dozen secondary schools, and fifty-odd elementary schools. The non-Adventist enrollment in these schools generally exceeds 50 percent at the elementary and secondary levels. Welfare programs are established in most local churches, and there are welfare centers in the larger islands. Disaster relief has been one of the most successful aspects of welfare assistance. Youth programs include the usual range of church associations for religious and recreational purposes as well as groups which closely parallel scouting. Youth organizations are divided into age grades which span from early childhood to about age thirty.

Hence while lacking a secular calling in the Calvinist sense, Adventists are driven by the urgency of a Work which makes secular social reform a part of its evangelistic thrust. Although the entire world is not a monastery, those spheres of worldly activity in which the church is involved are a legitimate setting for morally meaningful conduct. The social mandate of Adventists is thus narrower than that known to the early Calvinists, but is a mandate nonetheless. Perhaps through the Work Adventism will function to encourage a type of development that is more humane and community-oriented than that promoted by the earlier fruits of the Reformation.

Two concluding observations seem appropriate. First, Seventh-day Adventism can be profitably viewed from a Weberian perspective, despite its notable differences from the Calvinist prototype. An understanding of the calling and its social implications is a valuable reference for assessing the significance of prophecy, law, and church within a modernization framework. Second, in analyzing Adventism (or any religion) we must give careful attention to the dominant symbols that formulate both cosmic conceptions and ethical demands. In laying bare the meaning of these symbols we gain awareness of the processes through which belief systems become social forces in a field of action.

NOTES

Field research on which this paper is based was conducted in 1972 and 1973 with the support of the Institute of Social and Economic Research at Memorial University of Newfoundland. For helpful comments on an earlier draft I am grateful to Raoul Anderson, Rex Clark, John Kennedy, Lyndon McDowell, and James Peacock. I also wish to thank my wife, Gail, who assisted with the tabulation of statistical data, and Judy Bickford, who typed the paper for publication.
[1]My knowledge of the Adventist belief system comes from the oral accounts of both ministers and laymen and from various written sources. The book *Questions on Doctrine* (1957) is an authoritative and lucid compendium of Adventist teaching.

[2]This and other scriptural quotations are taken from the authorized King James Version, the edition of the Bible most commonly used by Adventists.

[3]The survey population consisted of fifty male Barbadian Adventists whose life histories I collected on tape in 1972. Respondents ranged between twenty and seventy-eight years of age, and generally represented a cross-section of the Adventist membership.

[4]Adventists identify their baccalaureate institutions as colleges. This causes some confusion in the British Caribbean, where baccalaureate institutions are called universities, the term college being given to sixth-form centers.

REFERENCES

Barbados Population Census 1970 (Bridgetown, Barbados: Government Publication).

Bellah, Robert, 1965. Religious Evolution. In *Reader in Comparative Religion,* 2nd ed., William A. Lessa and Evon Z. Vogt, eds. (New York: Harper and Row), pp. 73-87.

Geertz, Clifford, 1966. Religion as a Cultural System. In *Anthropological Approaches to the Study of Religion,* Michael Banton, ed. (London: Tavistock Publications), pp. 1-46.

Herndon, Booton, 1960. *The Seventh Day* (New York: Harper and Row).

Hill, Carole, 1973. Black Healing Practices in the Rural South. *Journal of Popular Culture* 6:849-853.

Keber, Helen Phillips, 1971. Higher on the Hog. In *The Not So Solid South,* J. Kenneth Morland, ed., Southern Anthropological Society Proceedings, No. 4 (Athens: University of Georgia Press).

Peacock, James, 1969. Mystics and Merchants in Fourteenth Century Germany. *Journal for the Scientific Study of Religion* 8:47-59.

Questions on Doctrine, 1957. (Washington, D.C.: Review and Herald).

Smith, Michael, 1961. The Plural Framework of Jamaican Society. *British Journal of Sociology* 12:249-262.

Thompson, G. Ralph, 1973. Let's Talk it Over. *Caribbean Union Gleanings* 45:20.

Turner, Victor, 1967. The Forest of Symbols (Ithaca, N.Y.: Cornell University Press).

Weber, Max, 1958. *The Protestant Ethic and the Spirit of Capitalism* (New York: Scribners).

Wilson, Bryan, 1970. *Religious Sects* (New York: McGraw-Hill).

The Case of the Healthy Hindu

MICHAEL V. ANGROSINO

IN a provocative recent article, Peter Wilson (1974) describes the "dual value orientation" of the Caribbean island of Providencia. Like many colonial societies in general, and like most West Indian societies in particular, Providencia is characterized by simultaneous aspirations toward *respectability* and *reputation*. Respectability Wilson defines as the degree to which one approximates the manners, customs, and lifestyles of the local elite. Reputation is the autochthonous system which, while acknowledging different social statuses, fails to rank those statuses; it is based on the local expectations of achievement. Thus, reputation

is also a counterculture to respectability and all that respectability stands for. Reputation emphasizes egalitarianism and opposes class hierarchy. . . . It regulates social relations by exercising sanctions intrinsic to the relations themselves rather than by invoking external codes of law. A man's reputation is rooted in his fathering of children, which is the most important demonstration of his maturity and manhood. (Wilson 1974:44)

Wilson discusses the impact of these social systems with particular reference to Oscar, a local eccentric. Although people took pains to tell Wilson that Oscar was extremely intelligent, they also warned him that he was mad. Oscar is a man who has been incapable of coping with and internalizing the ambiguous social referents of the dual value system. He had early in life denied the attainable goals of the local reputation system, and in his unceasing quest for respectability alone had gone "mad." Among the manifestations of Oscar's madness is his ability to sneak around, often materializing in someone's home, from which he takes an object he likes and substitutes in return one of his own "valuables." In the course of this activity, Oscar picks up a lot of gossip, and since gossip is an important means of social control in the West Indies, his behavior is tolerated by people when he tells them about someone else (in that case, he is "intelligent"); but when that same person becomes the object of Oscar's gossip, then Oscar is "mad."

According to Wilson, any society is, in one sense at least, the result of a delicate balance between privacy and surveillance. In effect, "the search for identity rests squarely on the freedom of choice we can exercise in entering into and conducting relationships with others" (Wilson 1974:50). The more privacy one claims, therefore, the more of a threat he becomes to others because they lose their potential for controlling his life. A madman, in such a case, is he who lives in a totally private world which excludes the society at large. Even if his behavior is not overtly harmful, others seek to label him mad and harass him in order to reassert some power over his life.

Although a clinical psychologist might well objectively label Oscar's symptoms as schizophrenic, the anthropologist makes no such clinical assessments. Rather, he aims to define and explicate the sociocultural system in which a person can be labeled as deviant. While many anthropological specialists have been concerned with this question, the medical social anthropologist approaches it not only as a topic of research, but as a critical theoretical issue as well.

Turner's classic study of the Ndembu shaman Ihembi (1967:359-393), for example, demonstrates the straightforward notion that deviance (even certain types of physical illness) has both an etiology and a therapy rooted in a particular social context. But in addition, Turner also attempts to account for the power of the social structure to both cause and cure illness. His discussion of the role of symbols and his more generalized notion of society as a sort of ritual drama may not satisfy every medical anthropologist, but the attempt goes beyond the by now well-established connection between social factors and deviant behavior and asks the question "How?" in addition to "What?" Wilson's discussion of Providencia does the same. He not merely traces Oscar's madness to its social structural context (answering the question "What caused the madness?" with "The disjuncture between respectability and reputation systems in a West Indian society") but attempts to account for the meaning of the madness (answering "How?" with "People feel their authority threatened when an individual, unable to resolve a value conflict, retreats into a private and autonomous world; so they label him mad in order to reassert their power over him and to put him in his place").

Social structure is not a mass of arbitrary institutions against which the individual bumps his head in blind ignorance. Society not only structures thought and behavior, it also reflects the belief system of the people who create it. It is perhaps unwise to dichotomize ideology and social structure since the two have such a complex feedback relationship; but one can analyze the underlying belief system of a culture, and then see how that belief is actualized in behavior on the social level. This device seems particularly appropriate in considering a case of health-and-illness behavior, in order to investigate not only the social context of behavior but also what the behavior means in terms of the group's ideology.

This paper, then, will discuss a case of a significant and (partially) socially defined pathology—alcoholism—in another Caribbean society, the community of Indians originally imported to the island of Trinidad as indentured laborers following the emancipation of the slaves in the British Empire in 1837. Indians now make up approximately one-third of the population of Trinidad (Weller 1968; Wood 1968).

Most of the indentured Indians were of low-caste status, and all of the laborers, having emigrated overseas, were symbolically declassified by the Hindu injunction against crossing water, an act which washes away the ties of caste. Anthropologists and historians speak of the "dissolution" of caste among the Trinidad Indians (Schwartz 1967). However, to see the transformation of the structural aspects of the caste system as a dissolution of caste is to misunderstand the nature of that system, and to misinterpret the nature of the Hindu belief system, in which some 85 percent of the island's Indians participate.

To evaluate properly the role of caste in Indian ideology and behavior, it is necessary to remember that in India caste functions on two distinct, if interrelated levels. On the philosophical level, caste renders a rank order of ritual purity. According to the Hindu doctrine of *karma,* in which actions in a person's life are burdens on the soul that must be expurgated in another life, one's station in life has a moral value; a lowly position indicates unworthy behavior in a past existence. Thus, the higher one's caste, the more nearly purified one is. It is a significant feature of the Hindu value system that pollution can be transmitted (like disease) but purity cannot (Basham 1959: 151).

Beyond this ritual ranking, caste also serves a pragmatic socio-economic function. Each local subcaste representing the national caste in a given village or district is defined in terms of its hereditary occupation. One inherits not only that occupation, but an extensive set of service obligations to members of other castes in the village. This network of service relationships, known as the *jajmani* system, insures the economic integration of the traditional village. No caste is an oppressor, none a complete slave. Every group, from top to bottom, has duties to perform for everyone else, but duties must also be performed for it in return (Mandelbaum 1970:159-231).

Some anthropologists use the socioeconomic function of the *jajmani* system to account for the persistence of the otherwise inexplicable belief in caste.[1] Such a position points to the abandonment of the *jajmani* relationships on the Caribbean sugar plantations, where the economic system made those relationships irrelevant, as proof of the abandonment of caste. This functionalist view of caste is quite valid up to a point, but overlooks the ideological component that continues to have great force within the overseas Indian community, despite changes in overt structure, just as Indians continue to refrain from eating beef even in an ecology that could support the production of cattle for consumption (cf. Harris 1966).

By the same token, the moralistic and ritualistic aspects of caste retain their force even with the major reinterpretation of the socioeconomic *jajmani* relationships. Contemporary Trinidad Indians only dimly perceive their caste affiliations, and caste plays an increasingly minor role in patterning social interaction. Nevertheless, the social factor that the Trinidad Indian novelist V. S. Naipaul has called the "knowledge of degree" is "in the bones" of the Indians (1964:55). Perhaps because Indian history has seen many invasions by alien cultures sweep into the subcontinent, the Indians cannot view the universe as a stable, well-ordered, harmonious whole. Perhaps the extreme logic of the Indian philosophical systems, which emphasize numbered categorizations, stems at least partially from the Indians' need to impute some sort of order to the chaos around them. Although ultimately "everything is one" in most Indian philosophies, there is a multiplicity of manifestations of that oneness—many gods, many paths to spiritual liberation, etc. The recognition of multiplicity as the essence of oneness is part and parcel of the success of Hinduism in absorbing and adapting to outside influences.

The caste system is a social example of this cosmic order; although all people are one, there must be, by definition, many different types of people. Even when overt economic functions of caste become irrelevant, and even when the ritual distinctions of caste cease to play an immediate role in a changed round of ceremonial activities, the "knowledge of degree," the knowledge that groups of people *must* be different but that their interactions can be formalized and made less threatening, remains a factor in the social system of any Indian society.

"Knowledge of degree" is, then, the social aspect of the Indian philosophical concept of *dharma*, the moral order. As expressed most clearly in the *Bhagavad-Gita*, *dharma* is not a construct implying some sort of abstract and universal morality. Rather, it is morality expressed in the ordering of peoples, ideas, and events. Accordingly, it is better (i.e., more moral) to be a faithful untouchable than to be a mediocre Brahmin. By accepting one's place in the scheme of life, one affirms the essential order of the cosmic plan. Thus the notion of the caste system (or the more diffuse belief in "degree") rests on assumptions that are deeper and more powerful than economic pragmatism. To acquiesce to caste (an attitude that strikes the Westerner as passive) is not surrender, but an affirmation of the underlying ethic of the cosmic order. The Indian social system, even without the overt markings of caste, continues to be an actualization of the belief in differentiation (and formalized intergroup relations) as the route to ultimate oneness and release.

This framework for understanding Indian societies enables the medical anthropologist to analyze the public health problem of alcoholism among the Trinidad Indians. The Hindu sacred texts generally condemn drunkenness (excess of almost any kind, for that matter) although complete abstinence has apparently been neither an ideal nor a norm, save among professed ascetics. Nevertheless, India was not known as a drinking culture. If anything, drug usage, not alcohol, distressed the British colonial officers and Christian missionaries.

Upon translation to the Caribbean, the Indians, heretofore a people indifferent to alcohol, suddenly were set down in a society of drinkers. Liquor flowed in the sugar plantations. After all, from the omnipresent sugar cane came the rum which was available in such quantity and at such low prices as to make its consumption almost an economic necessity.

According to the recollections of contemporary informants, the Indians were not at first "molested" in their habits. Unlike the slaves, who were ruthlessly stripped of their language and culture, the indentured laborers were allowed to keep their culture as long as their practices did not interfere with the plantation routine.

One of the customs tolerated was *ganja* (marijuana) smoking. *Ganja* could be bought in company stores on certain plantations, and people today recall their grandparents saying that gathering together in a barrack common-room to smoke *ganja* and drift into revery was a just compensation for a day's hard labor in the fields. Ultimately, however, economic and moral forces conspired against the practice. Many planters began to cut operating costs by converting some of their bulky sugar into transportable rum and by including extra allotments of rum in lieu of cash salaries to the laborers. Willy-nilly the Indians were flooded with rum, and within a generation they had become even more notorious drinkers than the emancipated slaves.

Missionaries regarded this behavior with some disgust, seeing in it the further degeneration of the pitiable heathen. Although the rum consumption by the Indians (of both sexes, of all ages and of all stations) was heavy enough to have caused such dismay to non-Indians, nevertheless *within the context of their own society,* these people were not pathological, not alcoholic in the modern medico-psychological sense.

To understand why even extremely heavy consumption of alcohol did not constitute a problem for the estate Indians, it may be helpful to refer back to Wilson's model of Caribbean society. The dilemma of the black West Indian has been his need to adapt simultaneously to the respectability and the reputation systems, a case of a double and frequently contradictory enculturation process. The Trinidad Indians, however, confronted not only the existing dual value standards, but had brought with them their own ideological system. Unlike the slaves, however, the Indians were not pressured to conform to "socially acceptable" standards of behavior, and while they stayed on the estates, the indigenous dual system interested them only peripherally. Since, unlike the slaves, they were neither converted nor taught English, the Indians could look to the respectability system as a sort of distant ideal—one to be admired because of its association with the wealth and power of the plantation elite—but not one that had any direct bearing on their daily lives. At the same time, the Creole reputation system, although closer at hand, could be ignored because the Indians despised the dark-skinned Negroes and their lack of ancient culture. Therefore, in the first phase of Indian life in Trinidad, only their own value system was relevant.

For the Indian involved in the strictly Indian value system, proper behavior concerned merely the fulfillment of his own special place in society. Each individual existed within the protective custody of his own particular station in life, maintaining a built-in notion of privacy in Wilson's sense. Because of the deep-set Indian belief in a degree of separation among people as a social analog to the cosmic notion of oneness-out-of-multiplicity, even a heavy drinker rarely impinged on the privacy of any other Indian. The structure of their social relations already kept them at a ceremonialized distance. Moreover, Indian drinking in the estate days merely replaced *ganja* smoking and so enabled the Indians to achieve a quiescent retreat inward. In some cases, in fact, such as the ritual sealing of the marriage arrangement, drinking became a ceremonial bond among in-laws. Of course, heavy drinkers in those days, too, damaged their brains and livers and suffered the numerous other physical effects of excessive drinking; but they were not labeled pathological because they posed no threat to the structure of their own society. If the individual drinker was remorseful over some act he had committed while drinking, he could seek out the *pandit* (priest), sponsor a *kattha* (scriptural reading to which the public is invited), and thus express his repentance. The ceremony was not designed to cure his alcoholism, since in the social sense he was not suffering from a disease that required a cure at all. Most likely, he would be drunk at the *kattha* or shortly thereafter, but this caused him no shame; he had only to repent individual acts that overstepped boundaries—he did not have to seek therapy for an overall syndrome of behavior.

The turning point came during World War II when Trinidad played host to large numbers of American servicemen who guarded the island's oil refineries from German sabotage. After the economic limitations of the estate days (the plantations began to break up after World War I) and after the despair of the Great Depression years, the war and the Yanks' "occupation" opened up undreamed-of vistas of progress and modernity, ideals which still, to a very large extent, dominate the Trinidadian lifestyle. "Workin' for the Yanks" became a shortcut to liberation from the estates and provided the Indians with access to money and power, factors unattainable while the Indians remained content to stay on the plantations and keep their way of life pure. Young men in the early 1940's thus became the first generation of nonplantation Indians, and with them the alcoholism problem can be said to have begun.

One of the classic views of alcoholism associates it with modernization, in the sense that the conflicts engendered by rapid culture change cause people to seek solace in the bottle; such has presumably been the case among the American Indians. In Trinidad a clear-cut association exists between modernization and alcoholism, but in a very different sense. Among the Trinidad Indians, the modernization process involved the assumption of American customs and ideals, but without necessarily increasing the amount of liquor consumed; rather, the *meaning* of drinking changed within the culture. The shift from the appellation "heavy drinker" to "alcoholic" expresses a profound shift in both belief and social action.

The war years provided the Indians with their first interactions with the dual West Indian system. On the one hand, the world of respectability was no longer a distant ideal, but there for the taking by means of the Americans and their jobs. On the other hand, the Indians clearly saw that the long-despised Creoles, unencumbered by ties to an ancient tradition, had the first jump into the Americans' world, so that the Creole lifestyle could be seen to have a certain pragmatic value, albeit not necessarily a true appeal. The key to the reputation system, that is, paternity, had always been a strong motive in the Indian system as well, but the machismo behavior associated with it was quite new. During the war, the Indians picked up the loud, vigorous, boisterous public behavior of the Creoles and Americans, and this became the mark of a man's manliness. Simultaneously, a technical education became necessary to get a good job in order to provide children with a good education, to legalize a marriage, and otherwise to live up to the respectable behavior appropriate in the world beyond the estates.

The American occupation thereby provided a new model of drunken comportment, and a new reason to drink. One no longer drank to "turn off" and relax, but to "put brass on the face" and become a high-rolling man-about-town. But at the same time, a man "workin' for the Yanks" was involved in a new social network which could easily be damaged by improper conduct. The heavy drinker of the war years could impinge on the privacy of others (whose degree of distance from him was ambiguously marked) in a way that would have been impossible in the strictly Indian world of the estates. He became, in effect, an alcoholic, no longer able to maintain the boundaries between privacy and surveillance.

Because of this wartime experience, the Indians began using the American notion of alcoholism as some sort of pathology. In effect they began to consider a set of behaviors which formerly did not constitute a problem as a symptom of disease. A disease—even one like heavy drinking—requires some form of therapy, which heavy drinking in the old days did not. By the end of World War II, the Indians had assimilated, to one degree or another, three different ideological systems, and yet the structures of the society in which they lived still reflected the older world of the estates. They had not as yet been able to actualize their Creole or Euro-American ideologies in a viable social structure, and so the conflict between what a set of behaviors meant and the social situation in which these behaviors were played out further complicated the problem of alcoholism.

All three belief systems entail traditional methods of therapy to which the Indian alcoholic might turn. The prayers of the *pandit* are purely Indian, while the ministrations of the *obeah*-man (magic practitioner) are purely Creole. Membership in one of the major Christian denominations is also considered in and of itself therapeutic. The Presbyterian and Salvation Army churches, however, are associated almost completely with the old colonial elite, whereas the newer fundamentalist sects by excluding all vestiges of Indian culture may in some cases add to the burdens of being an Indian in a plural society.

The Alcoholic Treatment Center (A T C) at the government mental hospital specializes in alcoholism therapy, but although it has served thousands in its decade of operation, few regard it as a real answer to the problem of alcoholism. It ministers to approximately fifty patients at a time, almost all of them men; most stay for six to eight weeks to undergo detoxification. A selected few also receive aversion therapy. The former is by no means a cure, for a detoxified alcoholic is likely to be back on the streets, drunk, immediately upon release. Moreover, the A T C is a social isolate, set away in a private cottage on the grounds of the hospital, itself an enclosed compound set apart from the small suburban town of St. Ann's. For an Indian, to be shut up in a sterile, institutional atmosphere away from his family and village is more a punishment than a boon. Indian men also resent kitchen duty as part of their rehabilitation, for it gravely offends the Indian male self-image. The A T C, then, a fully elite therapeutic resource (as the *pandit* is thoroughly Indian and the *obeah*-man completely Creole), may provide temporary symptomatic relief, but no real cure.

Alcoholics Anonymous (A A), the final therapeutic resource, first came to Trinidad in 1957, introduced by a white Trinidadian alcoholic who had joined in the U.S. It currently has approximately five hundred active members plus approximately five hundred more "floaters" scattered among some forty groups in all parts of the island. This is the merest drop in the bucket when compared to the extent of alcoholism on the island. Nonetheless, A A represents the largest and most successful single alcoholism therapy agency in Trinidad and the most promising.

A A was founded in 1935 by the late Bill W., a once prosperous stock broker who hit the skids, but found God and a personal mission and lived to see his original idea of one drunk helping another expand into an international organization. The core of the A A program has remained basically unchanged since Bill first set forth his ideas and is expressed in the *Twelve Steps and Twelve Traditions* of A A. Briefly stated, the program revolves around the willingness of the alcoholic to admit—in public—his weakness and need for help. He surrenders his "tough ego" to the "power greater than himself" and devotes himself to staying sober "one day at a time." He joins his weakness to a group of people with similar weaknesses; out of that comes a collective strength. The group remains nonpartisan and only serves as a forum in which the alcoholic can find social support in his efforts to avoid "that first, fatal drink." Although one is never cured of alcoholism, one can learn to manage it; the controlled or recovering alcoholic thus carries the message to others "still suffering in the bottle" and thereby constantly reminds himself of the values of his own sobriety (Alcoholics Anonymous 1953).

A A developed in a white, middle-class, Christian, Middle American milieu, and yet it appeals to the rural, agrarian, poor, low-class Hindu Indians of Trinidad. This may be due to its essential cachet of respectability. It is as morally clean as the Presbyterian church of the mission era, and its injunctions about reforming one's life strike the same notes of moral rectitude as do the exhortations to progress on the part of the island's elite.

Unlike the A T C, however, the A A groups are not strictly an elite function. The groups operate in the villages and in neighborhoods of larger towns, participating in the local system of values as well as those of the elite. The groups meet in public places, and as a result A A in Trinidad is considerably less anonymous than the *Twelve Steps* indicate. In fact, just as everyone in a district knows who the "bad drunks" are, so they know who most of the members of A A are. Moreover, in Trinidad the A A member carries the message less by attraction than by promotion. The successful A A member often becomes a public scold, scouring the rumshops, seeking out erstwhile drinking partners in their homes, enlisting the aid of the drinker's family, distributing A A literature to all and sundry, all in the attempt to spread the gospel of sobriety. In orthodox A A literature, sobriety implies nothing more than the day-to-day abstention from drink, the first step in an alcoholic's moral and social reformation. But in Trinidad, sobriety signifies material as well as spiritual success. It also implies a Euro-American lifestyle, which Trinidadians often identify as the "modern" way of life, for spiritual purity necessarily brings material benefits, just as in the caste system a person's success in this life is correlated with his ritual purity. His newly acquired possessions are held to be not merely the result of the hard work a sober man can perform, but the necessary and just moral reward of the penitent sinner. The successful A A member, however, does not flaunt his material success for fear of incurring the *maljeux* (evil eye) of a jealous rival.

Like Hinduism (and unlike the A T C), the A A philosophy does not stress individual guilt. Although one must make amends to people who have been hurt during the drinking career, alcoholism itself is a disease and not a personal moral failing for which the individual is responsible. The Trinidad alcoholic finds comfort in being part of a modern (i.e., imported) therapeutic process, yet one that does not conflict with his underlying beliefs about the moral nature of the cosmic order. The penitent need not wait for divine mercy to respond to an abstract moral imperative, as in the Christian churches; rather, once the alcoholic makes his "admission" (by standing up at a meeting and saying, "My name is . . . and I am an alcoholic") he reaffirms his place within the proper social scheme of things and has a right to expect his just rewards immediately. Interestingly enough, the spectacle of a reformed alcoholic seems to be so edifying that A A members (who make a practice of announcing their affiliation to the district at large) are very frequently given a chance for good jobs, are considered to be trustworthy business partners, and do indeed become economic and social leaders in their districts. At least one member is an avowed "millionaire," and two are politically influential on the national level. Needless to say, such dramatic success does not happen in every case, although it happens just often enough to keep the belief alive that rewards do flow to the serious A A member.

In this way, membership in A A enhances the alcoholic's reputation among his peers as it grants him a measure of respectability in the world outside. The West Indian reputation depends, as Wilson points out, to a certain extent on a man's abilities as a talker—oratorical gifts per se are valued, regardless of content. Activity among drinkers in the rumshops is often more verbal than otherwise. Brawls are not unusual by any means, but verbal slugfests make up the bulk of a rum-filled evening. At an A A meeting, on the other hand, each member gets a chance to speak. In the U.S., only selected speakers fill an evening's program, but in Trinidad everyone present is called upon, if possible, so that meetings often last four or five hours. Each speaker receives a courteous and respectful hearing, even those who, in the opinion of the others, "talk a set of stupidness every blasted week." Several of the most silver-tongued A A members have become national stars, called upon to contribute to meetings of groups other than their own.

The A A meeting is very much like a "lime"—the male peer group which is the most important non-kin social group among the Indians. Two of the newer A A groups on the island were founded when the members of drinking limes converted all at once. Like the lime, the A A group provides unending support; everyone is theoretically equal, there are no "bosses," and each member may say what he pleases in his contributions, assured of a polite hearing. Perhaps because the A A group resembles closely the all-male lime, only three women participate actively, none of them an Indian.

If A A is a vehicle for achieving elite respectability and Creole reputation, it is an Indian "business" as well, as the members themselves describe it. Of the active membership 96 percent is Indian, and except for the four predominantly black groups in Port of Spain, all the others have adopted Indian customs. The A A philosophy, too, has been subtly altered to fit the Indian village setting. The weekly group meeting, in its arrangement of personnel and activities, parallels the *puja*, the basic household-blessing ritual of peasant Hinduism. During the course of a *puja*, the *pandit* leads the celebrants in a ritual building of a symbolic abode to invite divinity to enter the house. In orthodox A A practice, the chairman of a meeting is merely a functionary with no real power. The head of an A A group in Trinidad, however, although not a "boss," is frequently considered an elder statesman in the sense that his charisma has induced other members to join. Many of the most successful A A members have sponsored dozens of new members who maintain a personal loyalty to him as well as to the group; one of these sponsors says quite explicitly, "Being disrespectful to your sponsor is the first step back to the bottle." The sponsor, then, is like the *pandit*—a spiritual guide leading his followers on to the general blessing.

As has been noted, in the Hindu belief system, pollution can be transmitted, but purity cannot. The A A belief that the member is in chronic danger of "slipping" back to the bottle echoes the idea that the world is rife with potential contamination. Although the "saved" sponsor can no more than a *pandit* pass his purity on to his followers, he can provide a moral model to keep the faithful away from sources of pollution.

Indian society is considerably more private than Creole society in Wilson's terms. The "knowledge of degree" which separates groups of people from each other tends to create barriers to interaction, and rings with formal expectations those interactions that are possible. Part of the alcoholic's conflict arises from the lack of formalized status expectations in the Creole and elite systems and the consequent confusion about propriety of behavior. A A in Trinidad, in formalizing categories of behavior (such as the leader-follower relationship), adds a note of Indian stability to "modern" behavior.

Pictures of Bill W. and printed quotations from A A literature adorn the meeting room walls in iconographic fashion. The custom of opening the meeting with the A A "Serenity Prayer" fits the Hindu mood of sanctity, and the Trinidadian proclivity toward salting contributions with verbatim stock quotations from the A A literature adds a special *mantra*-like touch.

The highlight of the *puja* is the sharing of *parsad*, blessed food offerings which are passed among the visitors and distributed throughout the village to spread the blessing from house to house. The analogous highlight of the A A meeting is the coffee break, referred to as "the sharing of our fellowship." Members consider it more than a social conclave, seeing it as the time during which the spiritual benefits of the contributions are fully distributed by being talked over. A member who leaves the room "misses all the fellowship" and "might well not have come at all."

In addition to the weekly meeting, each group engages in two other types of meeting, both of which have analogs in Hindu ritual practice. The group's annual anniversary is very much like the Hindu *bhagwat,* which is essentially a household *puja* expanded to accommodate and feed upwards of a hundred guests. Just as the *bhagwat* spreads the household blessings to the community at large, the A A anniversary spreads the group's fellowship to all A A members in recognition of the interdependence of all members. Finally, A A groups occasionally sponsor open meetings at which nonalcoholic members of the community are provided with information about the disease of alcoholism and are told about the therapeutic work of A A. This is analogous to the *kattha,* the public scriptural reading designed for the edification of the community at large.

By these means (few if any of them consciously devised), A A carries the message of modernity and social activism—and health— within the familiar, comfortable forms of traditional Indian ideological and social arrangements. In this way, a social pathology arising out of the conflicts inherent in adapting a society to a tripartite belief system is resolved in a therapeutic institution responsive to all three.

NOTE

[1]See Tyler (1973, ch. 8) for a concise explication of the socioeconomic functions of the *jajmani* system.

REFERENCES

Alcoholics Anonymous, 1953. *Twelve Steps and Twelve Traditions* (New York: Alcoholics Anonymous World Services).

Basham, A. L., 1959. *The Wonder That Was India* (New York: Grove Press).

Harris, Marvin, 1966. The Cultural Ecology of India's Sacred Cattle. *Current Anthropology* 7:51-66.

Mandelbaum, David G., 1970. *Society in India,* vol. 1 (Berkeley: University of California Press).

Naipaul, V. S., 1964. *An Area of Darkness* (Harmondsworth, England: Penguin Books).

Schwartz, Barton M., 1967. The Failure of Caste in Trinidad. In *Caste In Overseas Indian Communities,* Barton M. Schwartz, ed. (San Francisco: Chandler), pp. 117-148.

Turner, Victor, 1967. *The Forest of Symbols* (Ithaca, N.Y.: Cornell University Press).

Tyler, Stephen A., 1973. *India: An Anthropological Perspective* (Pacific Palisades, Cal.: Goodyear).

Weller, Judith Ann, 1968. *The East Indian Indenture in Trinidad,* Caribbean Monograph Series No. 4 (Rio Piedras, P.R.: Institute of Caribbean Studies, University of Puerto Rico).

Wilson, Peter J., 1974. Oscar: An Inquiry Into Madness. *Natural History* 83 (2):43-50.

Wood, Donald, 1968. *Trinidad In Transition: The Years After Slavery* (London: Oxford University Press).

Ritual as Communication and Potency: An Ndembu Case Study

Victor W. Turner

In a paper presented at a symposium on the "ritualization of behaviour in animals and man," Dr. Edmund Leach (1966:403) stressed first, as distinct from the ethologists' definition of ritualization among animals, that anthropologists are dominantly concerned with forms of behavior that are *not* genetically determined. He then went on to classify such behavior into three main types. These were:

(1). Behaviour which is directed towards specific ends and which, *judged by our standards of verification,* produces observable results in a strictly mechanical way . . . we call this "rational technical" behaviour.

(2). Behaviour which forms part of a signalling system and which serves to "communicate information" not because of any mechanical link between means and ends but because of the existence of a culturally defined communication code . . . we call this "communicative" behaviour.

(3). Behaviour which is potent in itself in terms of the cultural conventions of the actors but *not* potent in a rational-technical sense, as specified in (1), or alternatively behaviour which is directed towards evoking the potency of occult powers even though it is not presumed to be potent in itself . . . we can call this "magical" behaviour.

Leach proposes to class (2) and (3) together as "ritual," rather than to reserve the term, as most anthropologists do, for behaviors of (3) only. In this way he hopes to call attention to the highly important functions of ritual—including religious ritual—in preliterate societies of storing and transmitting information.

I find this way of looking at the data extremely useful for certain purposes, for I have long regarded the symbols of ritual, which are its constituent units, in what might be called their cognitive aspect, as bins or storage units into which is packed the maximum amount of information. Symbols, in this regard, may also be viewed as multifaceted mnemonics, each facet corresponding to a specific cluster of values, norms, beliefs, sentiments, social roles, activities, and relationships within the total cultural system of the community performing the ritual. In different contexts, different facets or parts of facets tend to be prominent, though the others are always felt to be penumbrally present. The total significance of a symbol may be obtained only from a consideration of how it is interpreted in every one of the ritual contexts in which it appears, i.e., with regard to its role in the total ritual system. However, I hope to show that, although fruitful, this approach fails to account for the peculiar efficacy felt by believers to attach to the ritual of class (3) in Leach's typology. It helps us to understand the cognitive, but not the affective and conative aspects of such ritual. The distinction between (2) and (3) is still a significant one. Leach, in his typology, gelds ritual, (if you will pardon the Jovian if not jovial metaphor); he reduces "potency" to "communication."

Each type of ritual, from the point of view of Leach's sort of information theory, represents a storehouse of traditional knowledge. To obtain this knowledge one has to examine the ritual in close detail and from several standpoints. In the first place the ritual is an aggregation of symbols. It is possible to make an inventory of these and against each to state its meaning. How the meaning is to be ascertained we shall consider later. For the moment let us suppose that it is possible to record, in fairly complete form, what each symbol signifies both for the average informant and for the indigenous expert. We then have a quantum of information, which represents a set of messages about a sector of sociocultural life considered eminently worthwhile transmitting down the generations.

We next have to consider what kind of information it is that we have revealed beneath the symbolic integuments, for the occasions on which transmission occurs are hallowed or sacred occasions, not just everyday events. The messages wrapped up in the ritual—and here, again, I agree with Leach that from the informational standpoint the distinction between verbal and nonverbal symbolic communication is unimportant—are messages from or about the gods or ancestors or daimones, and are charged with mystical efficacy. Our storehouse is also a powerhouse. In other words, we are dealing with information that is regarded as authoritative, even as ultimately valid, axiomatic. We are not dealing with information about a new agricultural technique or a better judicial procedure; we are concerned here with the crucial values of the believing community, whether this is a religious community, a nation, a tribe, a secret society, or any other type of group that couches its ultimate unity in terms of orientation to transcendental and invisible powers. We are not only profoundly concerned with values; we are confronted here too with relationships between values. In other words, we have to do with structure, not random assemblage. This aspect of structure emerges perhaps most clearly when we examine the liturgical or procedural form of ritual. When we do this we find that a ritual is segmented into phases or stages and into subunits such as episodes, actions, and gestures. To each of these units and subunits corresponds a specific arrangement of symbols— verbal or nonverbal, activities or objects. Symbols are interconnected, synchronically and diachronically, in terms of conjunction and disjunction, superiority and inferiority, alliance and opposition, identification and separation, and so forth. The nature of the relationship between two or more symbols is a valuable clue to the relationship between those of their *significata* which are contextually specified as important.

Underlying the observable structure of a ritual may be detected its *telic structure.* This term refers to the design of a ritual as a system of ends and means. Each phase, stage, and episode has its particular explicitly stated end or aim, and the end of one stage is normally a means to the fulfillment of the next, or of the ultimate end of the ritual. One may observe this purposive aspect of ritual very frequently in the process of construction of a shrine, and in the deliberate fashioning of a symbolic object. Such a shrine or object is an *entelechy,* the becoming or being actual of what was potential. A good deal of ritual activity consists of the manufacturing of certain key symbols, which represent, so to speak, the crystallization or actualization of the "work" put into them. Unlike the Marxian labor theory of value, however, in this case the value of the finished product (the Marxian "commodity" or the completed symbol or arrangement of symbols) cannot be measured in quantitative terms. The process of its manufacture is effected through a series of stylized acts and gestures, accompanied by verbal behavior such as prayers and petitions to supernatural beings, words of consecration, blessing, or warning, and each of these verbal, gestural, and kinesthetic symbols contains a wealth of meaning. This wealth is stored up in the symbol or pattern of symbols and is purely a product of the cultural conventions of the ritual actors: it is a set of qualities expressed in sensorily perceptible form. But a ritual symbol shares this much with the Marxian "commodity": it may frequently conceal beneath its integument a system of social relations.

The symbol is not just the product of purposive action-patterns (to use Nadel's phrase); it is the product of interaction between human actors of roles. Something of the character of this interaction adheres to the final symbolic form, or better, is encapsulated in it. This formulation holds true even when the construction of a symbol is done by a priest or ritual participant acting alone, for the role he or she occupies is always a representative one: in his ritual capacity the priest represents a social group or category, whether it be the total believing community or a section of it, and *a fortiori,* he represents the sum of its characteristic internal role-interactions. Furthermore, there is often present the notion that the symbol is made with reference to or on behalf of certain ultrahuman or nonhuman entities or persons, the gods or ancestors of the group, who are believed to give power or grace to the symbol and through it to its user. Generally, however, there is cooperation between role-players in the making of a symbol: one actor may collect the wood which another fashions into an image, while others yet may bless or consecrate it, while still others may bow down before it or hold it aloft in triumph or sacrifice before it. Clearly, the meaning of the symbol is bound up with all these interactions between actors in the ritual drama, for the symbol would have no meaningful cultural existence without this collaboration in collecting, shaping, consecrating, worshipping, sacrificing. What is sociologically even more relevant here is the fact that the roles contained in an institutionalized ritual role-set have direct or indirect connections both with roles found in other types of rituals and with nonritual roles. Thus it may be culturally stipulated that a role found in one type of ritual should be played only by someone who has played a specific role in another type of ritual. For example, among the Ndembu of Zambia only a person who has passed through the circumcision ritual may become a candidate in the ritual of the hunters' cults. A comparison of the two types in terms of symbolism and telic structure will then shed much light on the nature of both roles and of their interactions with yet other roles. It may also be sociologically illuminating to analyze a ritual role into components—using informants' statements and observations of the role in successive ritual contexts as the basis of such an analysis—and to investigate whether such components form part of different roles. Thus, one component of a male ritual officiant's role may also be found in the role of father as culturally defined, while another may be identical with a component of a headman's role. A third component again might even possess attributes of the role of mother in that culture, thus crossing the sex division. For example, Ndembu speak of the senior officiant in hunting ritual as "Mother of huntsmanship" (*Mama da Wubinda*). But where ritual has become highly elaborate, it is probable that an important component of the ritual expert's role will consist precisely in priestly expertise: knowledge of how to perform rites, sacrifice properly, interpret symbols, and validly pronounce prayers or formulae. Where this specialization is found in preliterate societies we have some measure of the degree to which religious relationships are becoming associational in character and detaching themselves from the matrix of the multifunctional kin group.

It is clear from the above that any type of ritual forms a system of great complexity, having a symbolic structure, a semantic structure, a telic structure, and a role structure. Furthermore, that type may itself constitute merely a part or subsystem of a wider system of ritual and perform a specific function with regard to the maintenance of that total system. Each of the component structures of a given type bears evidence of possessing innumerable links with other parts of the total system. For example, some symbols recur throughout the different types of ritual forming that system, ritual roles are repeated, certain crucial values are expressed in different parts of the system by different symbols, and some of the ends or aims of different types of rituals are often the same or are similar or overlap or are complementary. Often complete rituals will form an interdependent series. These multiple cross-linkages and sequences which combine the parts into a system are reinforced by the constant repetition of symbolic acts and objects within single types of rituals. Leach (1966:408) has commented on this repetitiveness, which he calls "redundancy," as follows: "The ambiguity latent in the symbolic condensation tends to be eliminated by the device of thematic repetition and variation . . . this corresponds to the communication engineer's technique of overcoming noisy interference by the use of multiple redundancy." The system as a whole is full of repetitiousness precisely because it contains images and meanings and models for behavior which constitute the cognitive and ethical landmarks of the culture. Furthermore it arrays these in terms of relational patterns which are themselves regarded as axiomatic for the religion's *Weltbild*.

I would now like to take you for a tour through the ritual storage system of what is at first glance a relatively simple sequence of symbolic activities, involving a few simple material symbolic objects, in a set of rites comprising a single phase of one kind of Ndembu hunting ritual, known as *Mukaala*. This example will exhibit fairly fully the properties of ritual I have been talking about. It will, I hope, disclose the semantic riches stored up in a paucity of outward forms. In the present case I was fortunate in being able to obtain interpretations of the ritual details from several members of the *Mukaala* cult association. These were all hunters who had been afflicted by ancestral shades who had in their lifetime been cult members with misfortune at the chase. The hunters had then had the rites of the cult performed for them, had subsequently been successful in the hunt, and, assured of ancestral favor, had entered the cult as its lesser practitioners, gradually advancing to full knowledge of its mysteries (*jipang'u*). The *Mukaala* cult is itself one of a set of five cults, collectively known as *Wubinda*. Each cult is devoted to the propitiation of hunter ancestors. These manifest themselves to the living in dreams, modes of affliction, and reputed behavior in five different ways and have to be propitiated by five distinctive sequences of ritual activities. Certain symbols and patterns of symbols are common to the five, but each has its idiosyncratic symbols, behavioral styles, mode of ritual dress, songs, and drum rhythms. It is the task of the diviner, consulted by a hunter when he has persistent bad luck, to name the specific mode of manifestation within the genus *Wubinda* in which the victim's angry ancestor has "come out of the grave" to afflict his kinsman. The shades are very touchy—sometimes they afflict their kinsmen because these hunters have forgotten them "in their livers," sometimes because they have broken the ritual interdictions laid on hunters, and sometimes on account of protracted dissension in the hunters' kin groups or villages. *Wubinda* was originally the province of hunters who used bows, spears, traps, snares, and nets, but later incorporated hunters who employed muzzle-loading guns traded into the interior in the late nineteenth century by African middlemen—Ovimbundu, Chokwe, and Luvale— in exchange for slaves, guns, rubber, and beeswax. Gun-hunters in these West Central Bantu peoples developed their own specific cult-cycle known as *Wuyang'a,* which consisted of a series of four rituals, each marking a grade of increased prowess in the chase. But since the pervasive idiom of Ndembu ritual is a dialectical sequence of fortune followed by misfortune followed by its cure through divination and performance of cult ritual leading to the restoration of fortune, the separate cults of *Wubinda,* in no set order, came to be interleaved between the graded rituals of *Wuyang'a.* By itself *Wuyang'a* represented merely a quantitative advance in hunting prowess; integrated with *Wubinda* it took on the character of a religious dialectic. Every positive advance was through the overcoming of a negative condition, and this negative condition was due to a failure in contact or communication between the living and dead members of the cult, represented by the breach of ritual taboos or of the norms governing the behavior of hunters toward their living kith and kin. Misfortune followed by remedial action drew the hunter more deeply into communion not only with his deceased hunter kinsmen but also with his hunter fellows— who incidentally were scattered over a wide territory even beyond the limits of the Ndembu tribe into Luvale, Kaonde, and Luchazi country. In other words, the hunters' cult had a pantribal, even an intertribal character, with some of the features of a major religion.

With this necessarily abbreviated account of its cultural setting, let me put what are merely the preliminary rites of the *Mukaala* cult under the microscope and squeeze as much of their meaning out of them as our techniques permit. First of all I will present the simple action schema of the rites. Then I will consider each episode and element in detail, giving its indigenous exegesis. Finally I will examine the wider social and cultural contexts of the preliminary rites of *Mukaala*.

The preliminary rites fall into two phases. In the first phase there are twelve consecutive stages or episodes. A hunter fails to kill animals with his gun or traps. He goes to a diviner. The diviner tells him that one of his deceased hunter-kinsmen has "caught him in *Mukaala*." He then follows the diviner's instructions and with his axe and hoe makes a clearing and platform on a large termite hill. He cuts and plants a forked branch of the *musoli* tree as a shrine in the clearing and places a stone at its base. Then he takes a lump of white clay or gypsum in his hand; invokes the *Mukaala* shade; and anoints the shrine elements, various parts of his body, and his hunting gear with the white clay. He whistles to arouse *Mukaala*. Next he goes home, instructs his wife to make a separate fire for him on which his food will be cooked, and sleeps that night. He awakes at dawn, goes hunting, and eventually kills a duiker, an eland, or a roan antelope. He then takes the lungs and blood, intestines and blood, head and blood, or the tibia and fibula of his kill—all portions tabooed to nonhunters—to the newly erected shrine. He then addresses the shade, thanking him and praising him. Afterward he pours blood on the stone and washes it with the blood. He washes the forked branch with blood and puts meat in the bifurcations. Finally, he goes home and divides the rest of his kill in the village according to traditional rules of meat distribution.

The second phase, which has five stages, begins when the hunter's luck repeatedly fails him again. He suspects that *Mukaala* has withdrawn its favor. When he does eventually succeed in killing an animal, he takes the blood, lungs, intestines, head, etc. to the shrine and addresses the shade as he did earlier. Then he divides up the meat as before in his village. Then follows a period of success at hunting. After ten or twenty kills, however, his luck once more deserts him, his "huntsmanship leaves him." He goes again to a diviner, who tells him that *Mukaala* is angry with him, because an unauthorized person has eaten the portions of game reserved ritually for hunters or because he has divided meat unfairly. To find his huntsmanship again the hunter must sponsor a performance of the *Kutumbuka* or public rites of the *Mukaala* cult. This phase ends when the hunter announces his intention of calling the cult members together to hold the rites.

This bald narrative tells us very little by itself. It indicates that hunters have a special status; that private ancestral veneration as well as public ritual have a place in tribal society; that the value of reciprocity is ritually expressed in the *do ut des* idiom of rewarding the shade with an offering in return for good luck at hunting; that meat distribution must be in accordance with customary rules; that the hunter is seen as a just provider; that white and red substances, white clay and blood, play an important role in establishing relationships between living and dead kin; and that a chancy and hazardous economic pursuit is invested with much ritual. All these things have been said, on the basis of similar observations, time and time again by anthropologists and specialists in comparative religion. Let us now go steadily over the path we have descriptively trodden, but guided this time by Ndembu adepts of the *Mukaala* cult, who will reveal to us many unsuspected features of the cultural landscape threaded by that path. From their interpretations we will begin to see how important are the functions of ritual, mentioned at the beginning of this paper, of storing and transmitting information for members of the culture possessing that ritual.

Let us look at the first step: "A hunter fails to kill animals." This cryptic phrase, often used by Ndembu, is itself a shorthand for a whole set of experiences hunters are expected to have in association with bad luck. One such experience is to dream in a particular way. Dreams of a certain type relate to ancestral shades and to their modes of manifestation. *Mukaala* is known in dreams by a distinctive mode of dress. One informant described *Mukaala* or *Kaluwi,* as he is also known, as follows: *"Kaluwi* has the appearance of a man wearing *mazang'a* on his arms, forehead, and legs. *Mazang'a* are ridges of fur that extend along an animal's back. Long ago Ndembu hunters used to wear them. *Kaluwi* is also spotted with white and red on his breast, temples, brow, knees, neck, and on his skull. I once saw him (in a dream) like that." Adepts of the *Mukaala* cult are also decorated with white and red spots during the rites, "to remember *Kaluwi."* The term *izang'a,* the singular form, also stands for "the place where a beast is cut up after a kill" (White 1957:79).

Other informants have told me that *Kaluwi* is sometimes covered with leaves—Ndembu hunters sometimes conceal themselves thus when they stalk game. They explained further that *"Kaluwi* likes hunter-adepts to wear skins or leaves." Hunters no longer wear skins and this ritual reversion to a traditional mode of dress illustrates a recurrent feature of ritual everywhere, the conversion of what was formerly secular dress into a sacred habit, as when today's Franciscan friar wears what was once the work-smock of the Assisian peasant.

But *Mukaala* manifests himself in other realms than dream. In the deep bush a hunter can hear him whistling. His whistling (*muloji*) drives away the herd of antelope the hunter is stalking. Another practice of his is to jump on the back of the leading beast of the herd and goad it with his heels to run, thus drawing the herd away from the advancing hunter. Again, like Robin Goodfellow in the English folk tales, he may appear as a marsh light and lure a hunter into a swamp.

One informant gave me a list of the attributes of *Mukaala,* under his name *Kaluwi,* which is a usage of the Kaonde people of Luba origin, who live to the east of the Ndembu and were conquered by Lunda invaders several centuries ago. The Ndembu also represent a blend of Lunda conquerors and Mbwela autochthones, but whereas the Kaonde tribe in Solwezi and Kasempa districts largely retained their cultural identity and language, the autochthones conquered in Mwinilunga District were almost completely assimilated with Lunda to form the Ndembu people. *"Kaluwi,"* said this informant, "lives among rocks, mountains, and hills. Caves are his haunt. He is like the first people in Mwinilunga, the *Tunyika mavumu,* those who soften the skin of their bellies by rubbing (or 'pot-bellies'), who lived in caves and deep holes. When the Lunda came from Mwantiyanvwa's kingdom in the Katanga, these little people gave them food and then sang them a song: 'You have nowhere to sleep.' " From the description, these small, pot-bellied autochthones represented an older cultural stratum than the Mbwela, who are Bantu-speaking Africans. They may have been Pygmoid or Bushmanoid hunters now found no longer in the Ndembu area. Like them *Kaluwi* is said to be short in stature.

Kaluwi is further said to "like to dwell in high places," on hills and rocky spurs. He is also associated with large termite hills. He is compared with lions which "climb on large termitaries to see if there are animals about." I shall have more to say about this association with termitaries in a moment.

I collected a list of synonyms for *Mukaala* which throw further light on his cultural attributes. These synonyms also represent names taken by adepts in his cult. The most important of these is *Chibinda katili watili wuyaji nawukeleng'i.* This sonorous phrase means "hunter-trapper who trapped huntsmanship and chieftainship." It is a dense and elliptic set of symbols. For the term *chibinda* stands for the legendary Chibinda Ilung'a, youngest son of the founder of the second Luba empire in the eastern Katanga who wooed and won the Lunda princess Luweji Nkonde many centuries ago and sired the Mwanti-yanvwa dynasty under whose rule the Katanga Lunda tribal state blossomed into an empire. Chibinda had preferred hunting to ruling and went into voluntary exile from his Luba homeland, some say after a quarrel with his royal kin, taking with him a band of fellow hunters. He went westward to the Kalanye River where he met Luweji, who loved him at first sight and eventually made him her consort. Later he took possession of the royal *lukanu* bracelet, supreme insignium of Lunda rule, and Luweji's brothers and nephews, who should have succeeded to the kingship, went into self-appointed banishment and founded many other ruling dynasties among the Chokwe, Bangala, Luvale, Luchazi, and Luapula peoples. Thus the hunter who had eschewed chieftainship through his love of hunting, "trapped chieftainship." This theme of gain through loss is clearly linked to the ritual idiom of the West-Central Bantu, and more specifically to that of the *Mukaala* hunting cult.

It is hard to see why Bushmanoid autochthones are indentified with the supreme Lunda hunter-chief in the beliefs about *Kaluwi.* Perhaps a link may be found historically in the fact that the Mbwela who originally occupied Mwinilunga District are culturally and linguistically closer to the Luba, from whom Chibinda sprang, than the Lunda. The Kaonde, at any rate, who appear to have strongly influenced the cult, are of direct Luba provenance. Some of my informants regarded *Kaluwi,* the Kaonde form of *Mukaala,* as being a sort of emanation of Chibinda Ilung'a's personality. Chibinda is, for all Lunda, the archetype or epitome of the hunter.

Another synonym of *Mukaala* is *Kapwepula kamatung'a,* "he who is [in the form of] the wind [or breath] of the country." This has reference both to his whistling and to his invisible omnipresence in the bush. He is further known, in a phrase said to be Chikaonde, as *Chendela haluwanza mukonkisha nyamapakwela,* "the one who walks in a cleared or exposed place [without trees, it was explained to me], the blower of animals, the one who walks." Another of his names is *Lukombu mwenitanda,* "the leaf-brush, owner of the country," the last term being once more in Chikaonde. Finally, he may be called *Monganyama,* "the deceiver [as to] animals." This was interpreted to me as follows:

Monganyama is the cause when a hunter in the bush sees something moving about just like a duiker antelope and begins to stalk it. When he approaches he finds that it is just a termite hill, not an animal. The hunter stands still and thinks: "I was imagining that there was an animal moving, but I wonder to see that it is not an animal." Then he goes on and sees something like a snake. He cries out, "Oh, this is a snake!" and leaps aside. But it is only a long stick, not a snake. The hunter begins to think that an ancestral shade (*mukishi*) has caught him. That night he dreams that *Monganyama* comes and tells him that he is the one responsible for those deceptive appearances.

Incidentally, the term *monga* is derived from the Chiluvale verb *konga,* "to deceive." This fact underlines the intertribal character of the cult, mentioned earlier.

Indeed it is very probable that the concept of *Mukaala* is syncretistic, deriving historically from a variety of cultural sources—Lunda, Luba, Kaonde, Luvale, Mbwela, and Chokwe. It is also syncretistic in a structural sense. For the notion of *Mukaala,* and indeed of kindred manifestations of ultrahuman powers, seems to represent a compromise formation between an ancestral cult and a cult of nonancestral or "nature" spirits. A specific, named ancestral shade is said to "come out" or "come through in *Mukaala,"* or "in the form of *Kaluwi."* Some informants have told me that *Mukaala* is an *ihamba* (a term which among the neighboring Chokwe represents a species of nature spirit) which is called up by the shade of a hunter's deceased kinsman— either on the father's or mother's side—and that both kinds of spirit then jointly afflict the hunter. But this is a rare view, and, I suspect, a piece of rationalization. Although it is not stated in this way, the implicit belief of Ndembu is rather that *Mukaala* is a sort of corporate personality comprising all the dead members of the cult lined up behind a recently deceased hunter who most intelligibly and immediately represents them to a specific living hunter. Another way of putting it would be to think of *Mukaala* in similar terms to those in which Ndembu think of the masked dancers in their circumcision rites. These are regarded as the "dead of long, long ago," though each mask is dedicated to an important remote ancestor whose name is still remembered. When a circumcised Ndembu who knows how to portray the behavior deemed appropriate to each mask dons it, he becomes the concentrated essence, as it were, of some aspect of generalized ancestorhood coupled with analogous attributes of nature—their ferocity, geniality, fertility, authority, punitiveness, and so forth.

But the beliefs about *Mukaala* are of sociological, as well as of historical interest. For *Mukaala* represents all that is not part of the structured order of Ndembu society. In some respects, as we have seen, he stands for the now-vanished autochthones, the *Tunyika mavumu,* who once owned the land as a hunting resource and not in its cultivable capacity. As such, he does not represent any specific segment of traditional Ndembu society, whether conceived in terms of political, kinship, or territorial organization. He stands for the air men breathe, for the open and high land, for the caves that penetrate the earth itself. He stands for the broad intertribal hunters' domain, and within that domain, mostly for the open country, for the plains on which herds of antelope are found, for the swamps into which men may fall, for the rocky outcrops and hills. In this he contrasts with other manifestations of hunter shades, such as *Mundeli,* who is attached to the gallery forest along the banks of rivers and streams, and *Ntambu,* who haunts the deciduous forest, the bushland proper. He stands for much that is not ordered, for the unrestricted component of existence. The spots of red and white paint that represent him in ritual are analogous to those found in divination beliefs where they stand for doubt and obscurity, and for the haphazard as opposed to the systematic. Thus a diviner will not eat meat from a spotted animal, as this is likely to confuse his insight and cause ambiguity in his interpretations. *Mukaala* is, indeed, a deceiver, a sort of trickster figure, like *Elegba* among the Yoruba and Fon of West Africa. He hoodwinks and misleads. Likewise, he is a stranger, a Luba, like Chibinda Ilung'a, a Kaonde spirit, a Luvale, someone from outside *ordered* Ndembu society, yet playing a key role in Ndembu *culture*. He is an autochthone, a troglodyte, before and below Ndembu society, and simultaneously, an outsider to it. He cannot be pinned down, he is capricious, arbitrary, fitful, a will-o'-the-wisp, mischievous, dangerous. He is a master-symbol of the accidents, perils, and disappointments of the hunter's life. Yet at the same time he can be propitiated, even to some extent controlled, by performance of the proper rites. And if you get him on your side, he can be a source of great blessings—he can help you to slay many animals. What he seems to require is something like a total commitment to the hunter's way of living; a hunter must identify with him, take one of his names, become as fluid, mobile, and unattached as he is. If the hunter can't beat him, he must join him.

These comments on *Mukaala* beliefs may help us to understand some of the *Mukaala* practices. Let us pass over the divination seance—the broad lines of which I have described elsewhere (Turner 1961)—and examine the ritualized space the afflicted hunter creates for himself in order to communicate with *Mukaala.* As we do this we will closely scrutinize his verbal and nonverbal behavior, as well as the symbolic articles or objects he assembles and arrays.

First of all, the hunter hews and hoes a cleared space on a big termitary. Such a clearing is known as *mukombela.* According to White's *Lunda Vocabulary* (1957:33), this means "a cleared spot (as for invoking spirits and setting traps)." Etymologically it is a most interesting term. It is derived from *kukomba,* "to sweep or clear up litter." From this verb is formed the verb *ku-kombela,* "to invoke spirits." The primal situation of ancestral invocation is at the *muyombu* trees planted in villages as shrines to the shades. When an Ndembu elder wishes to invoke the help of a shade, he first sweeps the earth at the base of the tree planted to that shade. He does this in order to sweep away "impure things" or *tububu,* which literally means "insects," but is here a euphemism for familiars or creatures of sorcery. Impurities may be caused by breaches of ritual interdictions, consciously or unconsciously motivated. The belief underlying the sweeping is that one can only approach the shades with any hope of being heard by them if one is both ritually and inwardly "white" or "pure." For this reason both the shrine-tree and the invoker are anointed with white clay, which is both an instrument and an expression of pure intention. The ritual action of sweeping is an aspect of the same religious theme. Other expressions of this theme are represented by abstinence from certain foods or from sexual intercourse for variable periods before approaching the shades. Sweeping, however, is not solely to purify; it is also to demarcate. It is to set off a portion of the visible and tangible world from the rest of it for the purpose of approaching entities that are normally invisible, though they may appear in dreams of the night, that realm of the occult and unseen. Thus one of the Ndembu terms for "the sacred" is *chakumbadyi,* "that which is aside" or set off from the everyday world. Into the concept of *mukombela,* too, goes the sense of an area cleared to make a trap or snare. Here it will be recalled that Chibinda, the archetypal hunter, "trapped or snared huntsmanship" (*watili wuyaji*). The hunter wishes, by this action, to begin to catch again the huntsmanship which has fled from him. Elsewhere I have discussed (Turner 1968:82-86) some of the semantic foundations of Ndembu symbolism and mentioned the etymological or nominal basis of meaning, together with the substantial basis—the raw material used for the symbol—and the artifactual basis—the finished symbolic product after it has been shaped or tooled for ritual use. In *mukombela* we have a vivid expression of the etymological component in religious symbolism—a component that is present in ritual everywhere. It is a form of serious punning, a homonymy indicative of the regular tendency of religious and indeed aesthetic and poetic symbols to synthesize, identify, and concentrate significations that are otherwise carefully segregated. This is a semantic procedure antithetical to that of logic and scientific definition, which seek to attach to a concept a single meaning only. But it has the economic advantage in preliterate society of storing up a wealth of information in a few visible signs. These have the function of mnemonics which can be elucidated by experts or adepts in the religious culture and explained to the novices or neophytes as they undergo their rites de passage from the practical-empirical domain into the sacred world, where the crucial values of the culture are linked with sensorily perceptible objects and activities defined as *sacra*. Finally, as one informant told me, a *mukombela* is made "to please the shade; formerly it was not well-known, now it is well-known." By clearing a space to venerate the shade, the dead hunter is removed from obscurity and brought to the attention of the living again. Moreover, in the clearing, the shade is given offerings of blood and meat by his living kin—he is literally nourished by them.

We now have to inquire into the meanings attributed by Ndembu hunter-adepts to the other components of the shrine built to communicate with and honor *Mukaala*. These are: the large termite hill, the forked branch, and the stone. One informant told me that "termitaries, large and small, are symbols (*yinjikijilu*) of the shades (*akishi*) of hunters—hunters are buried there." For the Ndembu, termitaries are divided into two main categories, the large *tuwumbu* (sing. *kawumbu*) which may rise to a height of fifteen feet or more and are dotted about everywhere in the bushland; and the small *mafwamfwa* (sing. *ifwamfwa*), normally about a foot in height, found everywhere in the bush and even in some of the open country. The latter have innumerable ritual uses and are mentioned in folktales. Great hunters are buried in the large ones, sitting upright with a large straight branch (*kanenga'neng'a*) of a species of tree known as *mudyi,* placed parallel to his brow so as to emerge from the grave. Offerings of blood are poured down this by his living hunter kin. It was not reported to me but I suspect that the clearing in the rite we are now considering is made on the grave of the actual hunter whose shade has been divined to have "come out in *Mukaala*" to afflict his junior kinsman.

If we now shift the focus of our attention temporarily from the *Mukaala* ritual to the total ritual system of the Ndembu and consider it in terms of the basic classifications it contains, somewhat in the manner of Durkheim and Lévi-Strauss, we find that the large termitary is one expression of a general principle, that of elevation, which is opposed to what is low, commonplace, or of humble rank or position. For example, chiefs are sometimes spoken of as *tuwumbu,* and indeed, I well remember the perturbation among the Ndembu caused by the death of an incumbent of the Mwantiyanvwa Paramount chieftaincy in the Katanga, the fountainhead of chieftaincy for Ndembu as of all people of Lunda stock, who had taken the name Kawumbu on his installation. For the Ndembu, huntsmanship like chieftainship has great prestige, high dignity. They employ the phrase *kudilemesha kwa Wubinda,* literally "making huntsmanship heavy or worthy of respect," to express the characteristic attitude toward hunters by the rest of the population. It is for this reason that hunters bury their dead members in an upright posture and not lying on one side in the fetal position as ordinary villagers are buried. The hunter's corpse, in his termitary, is believed to look out over the bushland where he formerly roamed in search of game. He is above ordinary men as well as outside their ordinary life.

Small termitaries form important components of shrines set up to hunters' shades in or near villages or whenever rites are performed to propitiate and extol them. I have discussed their significance in other contexts (e.g., Turner 1962:52-53) but something should be said of them here, for in *Mukaala,* as in other hunters' rituals, they form part of the shrine set up in the cleared space. This shrine typically consists of a forked branch, known as *chishing'a,* around which, below the first fork, is twisted a braid of grass known as *kaswamang'wadyi.* At the base of the branch is placed a piece of small termitary shaped into a cube. Sometimes the branch is inserted in a hole in this cube. The termitary is here known as the "little hut of the shade" (*katala kamukishi*). The shade is thought to visit its "hut" during and after the rite. In other nonhunting rituals, such as circumcision and funerary rites, these small finger-shaped termitaries have an explicitly phallic significance. The swarming life within them is pointed out as a sign of procreative power (*lusemu*). In the past a hunter was buried with his face exposed and around his head was placed a ring of small dome-like termitaries, made by one species of white ants. An opening was made in this ring so that the hunter could "see through them clearly." Thus, in terms of Ndembu traditional exegesis, termitary symbolism contains reference to burial practices peculiar to hunters, to their vigilance, and to the feeling that their proper home is in the bush (represented by the termitary "hut") rather than in the village. Besides these senses there are overtones of fertility and virility from the wider context. These are further exemplified in a traditional hunters' song, one part of which runs: "We want [this man] to be a great thief of a hunter [i.e., one who steals animals from the bush], a man who sleeps with ten women in one day." The theme of uprightness—represented by the hunter's burial posture—also has ithyphallic connotations of virility and potency, as similar symbolism in the Ndembu circumcision rites indicates. In this matrilineal society, in which succession to office, inheritance of property, and prior rights to residence are through women, the continuity and structure of the social system are connected most vitally with the female principle. Men owe their elevation to chieftainship and village headmanship and their membership in structured lineage groups to their links with women. But hunting is preeminently a masculine pursuit. Masculinity is, as it were, banished to the bush and to the circumcision camp. But there it develops an autonomous focus and in the rites of the hunting cults, to which many hunters are drawn, one finds a great proliferation and concentration of masculine symbols. The ritual importance of hunting may perhaps be seen as "overdetermined" (to use the depth psychologists' term) by the masculine exclusion from the basic structural continuities. Indeed, even into this male realm the notion that social continuity is a female matter intrudes. For the great hunter ritual officiants, who are the trainers of junior hunters, are known as *amama a Wubinda,* "mothers of huntsmanship." Hunting, unlike pastoralism, which in Africa is also a dominantly masculine concern, does not produce an inheritable form of property which can be corporately managed, manipulated to establish ongoing relationships, both corporate and individual, and which multiplies as time goes on. Hunting is a hazardous pursuit, its rewards are ephemeral, and its orientation is toward the present rather than the past or the future. The hunting cults acquire time depth through ritual alone, not through a mutually reinforcing combination of biological, economic, legal, and ritual components. In hunting so much depends upon chance and individual prowess—yet because so much of the cultural importance of masculinity is associated with it, hunting has become, one might say, disproportionately invested with ritual to make it something like a counterweight to matrilineal descent.

Now let us take a closer look at the meanings assigned by Ndembu to the forked branch shrine, the *chishing'a.* Such branches are taken from several species of trees, all of which are said to be termite-resistant and to have a "strong wood," representing the strength (*wukolu*) of huntsmanship. From none of these species can bark string be made, and this is important in Ndembu eyes, for the use of such species, say Ndembu, would "tie up" (*ku-kasila*) huntsmanship. The prongs of the extremities of the branches are sharpened by hunters' knives, to impart to them the sharpness or acuity of huntsmanship—as informants say, "huntsmanship is sharp with power" (*Wubinda wawambuka nang'ovu*). The whiteness of the exposed wood of all the species used is also significant. Whiteness, in Ndembu culture, has many connotations; relevantly for huntsmanship these include strength, health, good luck, ritual purity, authority, good will between the shades and the living, the clear and known as opposed to the obscure and unknown, life, power, breast milk, and seminal fluid.

In the *Mukaala* rites one species of tree is employed in the manufacture of the *chishing'a*. This is the *musoli* tree (*Vangueriopsis lanciflora*), and its ritual significance is drawn both from those of its natural properties that are regarded as striking by the Ndembu and from its name. The *musoli* has fruits that fall in the early rains and draw many woodland antelope to feed under it. Ndembu say that this is how it gets its name, which they connect with *ku-solola*, "to make appear" or "reveal." Thus in the tree is the power (*ng'ovu*) of making visible or evident. In hunting rites it is believed that this power will be transferred to the hitherto unlucky hunter, many animals will be brought to his traps or weapons. They will be manifested to him, instead of remaining concealed in the bush.

The braid of grass called *kaswamang'wadyi* means literally "that which hides the bare-throated francolin." It is mentioned in one standardized invocation from the *Wuyang'a* gun-hunters' cult, which runs as follows: "Today this grass is the concealer of the francolin, in which all the animals and birds in the bush hide themselves. If an animal is concealed in the grass, may we hunters be swift to see it, that we may shoot and kill it, and be well pleased. May we carry it back and eat its meat. Do not (o hunter's shade) hide it from us. It must appear to view, you must reveal it to us quickly" (*muyisolola swayiswayi*). Here we find the by now familiar theme of "revelation" exemplified once more. But the use of this grass in ritual is to make the hunter invisible and his quarry visible.

This motif finds further representation. The twist of grass divides the *chishing'a* into two sections. Below it the shades are said to come to drink blood poured on the shrine as an offering. On the forked branches trophies of the chase are hung or spiked. "The hunters must resemble those shades," I was told. "The animals will not see them because of the grass." Thus the hunter will become invisible to animals, just as the shades of the dead are invisible to living men.

Finally, the stone (*ilola*) placed at the foot of the *chishing'a* is said to represent "the place of *Kaluwi,* who lives near rocks and hills." A stone is said, furthermore, to be hard like a hunter. Chiefs are also sometimes said to be "stones," meaning that they are resistant and enduring and hard with authority. In all these senses we find themes we have met before.

In one aspect, these symbolic objects represent features of the topography that have importance for hunters, for the *chishing'a* represents the forest; the *mafwamfwa,* termite hills, which play an important role in the food quest; the grass braid stands for grassy plains; while the stone images the rocky hills and outcrops. Here a complex whole is represented by one of its parts. When this composite shrine is taken together with the spirit manifestation to which it is devoted, one realizes forcibly how cogent is Lienhardt's (1961:147-148) interpretation of the "Divinities" or "Powers" of the Dinka, and how readily applicable it is to the Ndembu case. He discusses these not as "ultrahuman 'beings' which might form the subject-matter of a Dinka theology, but as representations or 'images' evoked by certain configurations of experience contingent upon the Dinkas' reaction to their particular physical and social environment, of which a foreigner can also have direct knowledge" and hence can at least partly apprehend. A Dinka "Power" or "Spirit" is not "an immediate *datum* of experience of the same order as the physical facts or events with which it is associated. To refer to the activity of a Power is to offer an interpretation, and not merely a description of experience." It may provide "a link between moral and physical experience, integrating experience of the human and the ultra-human in the world." A specific Power may be divined as the grounds of a particular human condition. Thus among the Ndembu *Mukaala* may be regarded, in Lienhardt's terminology, as "a subject of activity" within the afflicted hunter, which in the course of the ritual has to be isolated from him. *Kaluwi* or *Mukaala* (and the symbols which "body him forth") is an image of the experience of Ndembu hunters both in the bush and in the village. The misfortunes of the chase in woodland, plain, and hill at some point in the hunter's life come together and tally with disturbances in the social group—which as likely as not are caused by jealousies over meat distribution. This fatal union of moral and professional experience finds its interpretation in the belief that an ancestral shade, representing inter alia the sociomoral conflict, has "come out" in the guise or manifestation of *Mukaala,* the archaic and archetypal hunter representing the dangers and hazards of the hunting realm. Action can then be taken, in the form of ritual, with regard to an external image of inner feelings of guilt, fear, anxiety, and aggression aroused by social and psychobiological tensions and projected on the *Mukaala* stereotype. Since such experiences of combined moral and physical discomfort are common to all hunters, the cultural stereotype of *Mukaala,* a mosaic made up of many pieces of experience and derived from the beliefs of many hunting tribes, has in time become established as an important component of Ndembu religion. Yet it is through the experience labeled *Mukaala* or kindred experiences imaged as modes of ancestral affliction and the suffering and painstaking remedies these

entail, that a hunter has to pass if he is to achieve a valid commitment
to his culturally defined role. The man must be tempered by the experience to play the role properly.

Before we examine the ritual facts we have gleaned with the
help of indigenous exegesis in terms of the communication and storage
of information about experience and its cultural interpretation, we
have some further facts to consider. Whereas we have until this point
confined our attention to beliefs and objects, we have now to deal
with purposive activities, with what I have called the "telic structure"
of the rites. When the hunter has made his shrine to *Mukaala,* thus
defining the cause of his affliction, he anoints the elements of the shrine
and parts of his body with white clay (*mpemba*). He puts whiteness
by his eyes to see clearly, on his stomach that he may have food, on his
shoulders because he carries his gun and the meat of his kill on them,
and on his brow because his face should be "clean, white, or lucky."
The main aim of this action is to indicate that the hunter thereby
signalizes his intention of entering into full and honest rapport with
the ancestral shade and with the *Mukaala* form in which that shade has
emerged. He then invokes the shade as follows (I have several texts
of this type of invocation):

> White, all white is this *mpemba.* You my kinsman who have died, if you are
> the one who has come out in *Kaluwi,* now harken to me. Tomorrow when I go
> into the bush to seek for animals, you must cause me to see them quickly.
> I must kill animals by gun or trap. White is the *mpemba,* o my shade. I must
> be a fortunate person due to you. If my mother's brother's shade is here today,
> please let me have meat when I go into the bush. I must meet with an animal
> which is blind to me, like a Goliath beetle.

This last passage refers to this flying beetle's habit of blundering into
tree trunks and falling down like a blind being.

What is interesting about the kinship relations revealed in my
questionnaire[1] and further supported by observational data and narratives of rites by hunters is that in the hunting cults patrilateral kin
are fairly frequently divined as afflicting agencies. This contrasts with
the situation found in village rituals concerned with illness and repro-
ductive troubles, where only matrilineal kin are divined as the cause.
Here again we have an expression of the notion that hunting is a male
matter and that kin links through males are sometimes recognized as
links of intergenerational continuity in the ritual realm of *Wubinda.*

After the invocation, the hunter whistles, indicating his new rapport with *Kaluwi,* the whistling will-o'-the-wisp. He returns home and
his wife makes him a new fire on which his food will be cooked while
he is in a sacred state. This is a further instance of the symbolism of

being set aside from everyday life. The hunter is now in a liminal or marginal condition, betwixt and between the life he led before misfortune struck him and that which he will lead when he is lucky again. Liminal symbols follow thick and fast. The hunter goes off into the bush at dawn, which in many Ndembu rituals is regarded as a liminal period, between night and day, and is explicitly stated to be such by informants. It is considered especially auspicious if his first kill is a duiker. The skins of duikers are used in several initiation rituals, e.g., in the girl's puberty rites where on the first day the girl novice is laid on a duiker skin wrapped in a blanket to conceal her from profane observation. This rite too begins at dawn. Duikers seem to have some connection in a variety of ritual usages with liminality, perhaps because they tend to be inquisitive creatures who frequent the margins of villages—a fact often pointed out to me by Ndembu.

After he has killed, the hunter takes the lungs and blood, intestines, head, tibia, and fibula of the animal to his *Mukaala* shrine and addresses the shade again: "You have given me an animal. I have brought you its meat and blood too. You are the great hunter *Chibinda katili.*" He then pours blood on the stone and washes it all over with the blood. He washes the *chishing'a* forked branch shrine with blood and puts meat in its forks and impales portions on the prongs. Then he returns to the village and divides up the remainder of the animal according to traditional rules of meat distribution. This process of invocation, hunting, killing, thanksgiving, and distribution continues, as I mentioned earlier, until the hunter has another sequence of misfortune. When his huntsmanship leaves him, he goes once more to a diviner, who may tell him to sponsor the performance of a big public ritual, the so-called *Ku-tumbuka* phase of *Mukaala,* to propitiate the watchful and punitive shade.

Ndembu hunting rites and their traditional hermeneutics merit a monograph to themselves. Enough material has been presented, however, to discuss, rather more meaningfully than at first, some of the issues raised earlier in this paper. On the whole, Leach's view that the distinction between verbalized and nonverbal symbolic communication is unimportant from the standpoint of communication is upheld. The stereotyped interpretations of the alternative names of *Mukaala,* his allonyms (If I may stoop to a neologism), are consistent with features of the rites—he is said to live in stony places and a stone is part of his shrine, he is called "the one who walks in a cleared place," and a sacralized clearing is made on a termite hill. There is also a connection between the identification of *Mukaala* with Chibinda—the founder of the Lunda empire—and the stone in the shrine, for a stone represents chieftainship, and according to Northern Lunda tradition Chibinda and his royal Lunda wife used to sit on a stone and make loving converse before they were betrothed. Both verbal and nonverbal symbols have the property of multivocality, of having multiple meanings. Both relate to the contemporary terrain and to the remote past insofar as geography and history affect the experience of hunters. The allonyms of *Mukaala* have a further property of ritual language everywhere; they have both an archaic and a foreign ring. They are partly familiar and partly strange, at once intelligible and almost unintelligible. In other words, they relate mystery to fact, what is outside normal Ndembu experience to what is encompassed by it, what is unconscious or preconscious to what is conscious.

Here we might touch on two problems raised by ritual symbols of all types. Such symbols raise a problem of meaning and a problem of efficacy. The first takes us into the cosmology and ideology of the specific culture whose members operate the sets of symbols we are considering; the second raises problems for the psychologist, and may have universal human implications. I have often spoken of the bipolar character of the semantic systems associated with important ritual symbols—how one and the same symbol refers to values, norms, and ideals, and also to human physiological processes and phenomena such as coitus, lactation, blood, and sputum. Thus, in *Mukaala,* the composite shrine of pronged branch, braided grass ring, termitary, and stone has ithyphallic and coital connotations but also refers to the values and norms of a hunter's life, to kingship, to the ideology of the ancestral cult, and to the values attached to masculinity in the social order. What I have called the ideological pole of meaning is of interest to such scholars as Lévi-Strauss and Leach, who are concerned with expounding the "inside view" taken by the people themselves of their cosmos and society and how they came to be as they are, and with the systems of classification developed and utilized by the people. Beneath this "inside view," Lévi-Strauss, at any rate, would look for a universal structure of cognition, but would argue that before one can expose this structure one must strip from it the integument of specific cultural experience. This may well be the case but it is to the other semantic pole, the "orectic" pole, that we should look, in my opinion, if we are to gain a better understanding of how symbols influence the emotions of their users and fulfill their wishes. Here the reference to infantile experiences, autonomic processes, involuntary activities, in short, to the nonlogical and arational components of the human condition is probably crucial. And since the basic physiological experiences are experiences, in reality or phantasy, of relationships with others—in coition, lactation, anger, defecation and its control—usually in mating or nuclear familial contexts, we may perhaps see the semantic poles associated respectively with distinct types of social groups. The orectic pole—which is closely connected with the outward, sensorily perceptible form of the symbol—has links with the nuclear family with its deeply affectual ties, while the ideological pole is oriented more toward the wider society or political community. In bringing both the smallest and widest groups within the same semantic orbit, in identifying these tensed opposites in a gestalt, the important ritual symbols may develop in ritual action an awesome efficacy, since the abstract norms of the widest sociocultural unit are thus given charges from the primary human situations, while the objects and relationships in these, or their ritual equivalents, are given a greater degree of organization and turned, as it were, outward and away from their original objects to serve the ends of the total society.

Admittedly, I have not chosen a set of rites which obviously exemplifies this argument—life-crisis rites would have provided clearer illustrative material. But the hunting symbols of *Mukaala* and the verbal behavior I have described do represent a massive concentration of masculine attributes—both in their outward form—prongs, hard things, termite hills, killing, piercing—and in the senses attributed to them—huntsmanship, virility, chieftainship, strength, bonds between male kin (MB-ZS, F-S, EB-YB) and so forth. The ambivalent attitude toward the afflicting shade, who is now seen as a hostile, alien authority figure who punishes, and now as close kinsman who nurtures and blesses, is suggestive of experience in the primary group. But the attachment of these powerful affects, in symbols, to *significata* which represent values and norms shared by all Ndembu—fairness and generosity in distributing meat, openness and honesty to one's fellow tribesmen, sacrifice of a portion of one's kill to nourish the dead thereby indicating one's debt to the traditional structured order of society, and recognition of the common origin of all Lunda political unity in Chibinda Ilung'a, and the importance of reciprocity exemplified in such prayers as "You have given me an animal, I bring you its meat . . . that you may give me another animal . . ."—this attachment of small-group affects to large group ends and concerns seems to be a factor in accounting for the efficacy of certain key symbols. Such symbols are not only immediately moving—since they cue off orexis (appetite or desire)—they make ideas and rules moving too. And when, as often happens, the rules are directed against the very aggressive and libidinal drives to which they are linked within a given symbol's semantic structure, the resulting emotion experienced by the believer oriented to the symbol is a highly conflicting one—such emotion may be one of the components of Rudolph Otto's "numinous awe" and Kierkegaard's "fear and trembling" before the "religious paradox."

Thus if we are to begin to understand how ritual makes people tick, it is not enough merely to consider the symbolic molecules of ritual as informational storage-units. They are these and more, and in the "more" we move into the field of social dynamics where ritual both maintains the traditional forms of culture and becomes at times of major crisis an instrument for adjusting new norms and values to perennially potent symbolic forms and discarding old ones from the ideological pole of crucial symbols. What frequently survives major changes in the structure and organization of the wider society is the sensorily perceptible form of the crucial or focal symbol and its cluster of orectic or physiological references—as a glance at the major surviving rites of Hindu, Jewish, Christian, and Islamic religion will confirm. This may be because those references and that form originate in primary human experience in the nuclear family. The importance of these experiences is related to the perdurance of this unit and the tension between its independence from and interdependence with other units of the widest recognized social system. Ndembu hunting cults, in their symbolism, abstract the masculine attributes and relationships of the family on the one hand, and of the tribal group on the other, and exhibit these two sets of masculine components as a dynamic unity. Father and son, brother and brother, uncle and nephew hate and love and are reconciled; analogously, hunters and villagers hate and love and are reconciled. The processes within and outside the family are aligned within the structure of the ritual process, the ultimate aim of which is to enable the members of Ndembu society to think feelingly and feel coherently about their mutual relationships in hut, village, chiefdom, and bush. Symbolic activities and objects are thus more than components of signaling systems, they are switchpoints of social action.

NOTE

    [1]As the result of administering a questionnaire to ten Ndembu men, I found that out of nineteen instances of affliction by hunters' shades in various modes of manifestation, the angry ancestor in nine cases was divined to be the victim's mother's brother; in three, his own father; in two, his older uterine brother; in two, his classificatory mother's father; in one his mother's sister's son, i.e., a classificatory "brother"; in one his father's mother's brother; and in one was "unknown."

REFERENCES

Leach, Edmund R. 1966. Ritualization in Man. In *A Discussion on Ritualization of Behavior in Animals and Man,* organized by Sir Julian Huxley, Philosophical Transactions of the Royal Society of London, Series B, vol. 251, no. 772 (London: Royal Society), pp. 403-408.

Lienhardt, Godfrey, 1961. *Divinity and Experience: The Religion of the Dinka* (London: Oxford University Press).

Turner, Victor W., 1961. *Ndembu Divination: Its Symbolism and Techniques,* Rhodes Livingstone Paper No. 31 (Manchester: Manchester University Press).

----------, 1962. Themes in the Symbolism of Ndembu Hunting Ritual, *Anthropological Quarterly* 35:37-57.

----------, 1968. *The Drums of Affliction* (Oxford: Clarendon Press).

White, C. M. N., 1957. *A Lunda-English Vocabulary* (London: University of London Press).

Weberian, Southern Baptist, and Indonesian Muslim Conceptions of Belief and Action

JAMES L. PEACOCK

THE most systematic and comprehensive conceptualization of the relationship between belief and action is that of Max Weber. Weber's frame of reference (elaborated by such Weberians as Talcott Parsons) takes "action" (*Handeln*) as its fundamental unit, a feature which distinguishes it from other influential frameworks.[1] The Durkheimian perspective, which lies at the base of social anthropology, emphasizes the relation of belief to the social system, rather than to individual action. The Freudian perspective, which underlies the older type of psychological anthropology, emphasizes the relation of belief to the personality system. And insofar as cultural anthropology has any coherent perspective or emphasis at all, it tends to regard belief as part of a cultural system embracing worldview, values, symbols, and other shared understandings. For Weber, action is a unit of individual behavior, a set of acts plus their meanings, which form the building blocks for personality, social, and cultural systems and the raw stuff from which such abstractions are abstracted.

I should emphasize the phrase "plus their meanings." For Weber, an act is action only insofar as it has subjective meaning to the actor. And understanding of the action is impossible without understanding this meaning. Thus, Weber championed the so-called method of *verstehende Soziologie,* where the analyst endeavors to understand the action of the actor through formulating those purposes, norms, and beliefs which motivate, legitimize, and render meaningful his actions. For Weber, action could not be analyzed independently of belief.[2]

Starting from this theoretical position, Weber elaborated a rich typology of action in relation to the underlying subjective orientations. His most general scheme distinguished between *Wertrationalität, Zweckrationalität,* affectual action, and traditional action.[3] In the *Wertration-*

alität, the actor chooses his means in order to realize some single absolute value (*Wert*) without consideration of cost. In *Zweckrationalität,* the actor orients to a plurality of goals and considers the cost of achieving any one over against the others. The affectual action stems from instinct and emotion rather than a rational consideration of means, ends, and values. Traditional action simply conforms to custom rather than rationally considering the relation between means, ends, and values. In addition to formulating these general distinctions, Weber set forth substantive types in politics and religion. Political action can be charismatic, legal, or traditional. A leader may be obeyed because he has traditional authority stemming from custom and inheritance, because he has charismatic authority stemming from his personal magnetism, or because he occupies an office justified by law (Weber 1947:324-386). Religious action can be otherworldly or innerworldly, ascetic or mystical, to name two of the basic oppositions. The Calvinist-capitalist sketched in Weber's *Protestant Ethic and the Spirit of Capitalism* exemplified innerworldly asceticism: "mastering the world, [he] seeks to tame what is creatural and wicked through work in a worldly vocation" (Weber 1946a:325). The Buddhist monk is the opposite, the otherworldly mystic, and other combinations are exemplified by other religions analyzed in Weber's comparative *Religionssoziologie* (Weber 1951, 1958, 1964, 1967a, 1967b).

These types of action are what Weber termed "ideal types," a set of categories frequently misunderstood as the lazy man's substitute for statistical description. To define an ideal type, Weber first lays bare the actor's most fundamental subjective orientation, such as the ascetic or the mystical, then he postulates the pattern of action that would unfold *if* this orientation were logically carried out. No one realized more fully than Weber that the actual never corresponds perfectly to the ideal, but he believed that viewing the facts alongside the type would illuminate the patterning of action more powerfully than if one were simply to begin by describing the bewildering variation in observable behavior. What is repeatedly misunderstood about Weber's work is that in analyzing the phenomena of Protestantism, Hinduism, Confucianism, and the other religions he was struggling at once to illuminate empirical phenomena and to elucidate a system of types of action and belief. Failing to appreciate this heroically dual effort, philosophers persist in criticizing him as though he were merely a speculative theorist and social scientists as though he were conducting a Gallup Poll (see Samuelson 1964).

Seeking to help keep alive the Weberian tradition, I would like to follow his general approach in interpreting some data. I would like to develop a distinction between two types of relationship between belief and action, one exemplified by the Muslim Muhammadijans of Indonesia, the other by Southern Baptists. My observations of the first group were made between January and July 1970 primarily in Java, observations of the second come most directly from attending several Sunday night services in the Durham and Hillsborough area of North Carolina in early 1974. The Southern Baptist pattern[4] is familiar to anyone acquainted with evangelistic ,Protestantism throughout the United States and various parts of the world, but it is good to refresh memories by citing a few data. Names are of course fictitious.

A notable feature of the Southern Baptist evening service, which distinguishes it from most Southern Methodist, Episcopalian, and Presbyterian services on the one hand and joins it with evangelistic groups outside the South on the other, is the lengthy, intimate, and insistent *invitation* after the sermon. At Crusade Baptist Church, on a country road near Durham, the preacher is winding up his sermon, "Dare to be Different," by weaving it into an invitation for those who want to receive Christ or affirm their salvation to come forward to the altar. He speaks rapidly and soothingly into a microphone: "Just dare to be different . . . it's easy to stand up now, it won't be so easy tomorrow . . . [then contradicting himself logically but sustaining the emotional flow as he senses inhibition] I know it's difficult to stand up now, but Jesus stood . . . just come, come. . . ."[5] In the Northside Baptist Church near Hillsborough, a father and son have joined in preaching a revival campaign. Tonight the son has preached, and he concludes his sermon by asking those who want to receive Christ to come forward. Only three have come, a mother and a daughter whom she cradles as she leans over the railing in front of the pulpit and a young, dark-skinned boy (this church, like others to be mentioned here, is white). The preacher tells a story:

> There was a father who had a wild son. The father said, "Don't go out tonight." The son kept saying he was going until finally the father laid his body across the door, said, "you have to step over my body to go out tonight." But that's what that wild boy did. If you think that's terrible, what if you go forth tonight without receiving Christ. . . .

Then the preacher's father joins in the invitation, speaking in a more intense way (possibly to the anthropologist, or so he felt):

> There's somebody here who is caught by the devil, he wants to get loose, he wants to come forward, he should come . . . [then, finally, when no one comes] He was not able to come tonight, maybe he will next time. There will be no benediction, those who want to stay and hear the Smith brothers sing can, those who want to go may leave.

The invitation to receive Christ is, of course, not confined to the end of the church service, but is a major thrust, perhaps the major thrust, of the Southern Baptist faith. The invitation can come straight from God in a road-to-Damascus experience, it can be proffered in private by the pastor who encourages the sinner to get on his knees, and it is announced publicly by billboards which shout at us to repent, to be saved, to accept Jesus.

If the invitation is accepted, it leads to the experience of *conversion* as described in the sermon by the preacher of Northside:

There was a man down at Harnett County, he was known as a mean man. He was actually caught making liquor in a still while I was preaching a sermon on Sunday morning. There I was in the church, there he was in the woods only a few hundred yards away.

One evening I was sitting on the porch, the sun was just about down. This man came along in his pickup truck, he stopped and staggered out toward me. He was drunk, staggerin-drunk. I was scared. He was [now the preacher's voice rises to a thunderous shout] like the wild man of Gerasenes; he could break chains like threads. He said, "Let's go inside, I want to talk to you." We went inside, I was scared. It was dark in there, I didn't know what he'd do.

He started confessing his sins—all the ones I've told you about, like making liquor, bootlegging, and more, many more. The more he talked, the more down I got. I said, "It's bad. . . ." Finally, he said, "Preacher, what can I do?" I said, "Pray, ask *Jesus* for forgiveness." The more he prayed, the more up I got. He accepted Jesus.

When it was over, he said, "Get in with me." We got in the pickup, he had a ten-year old boy with him, he shoved him over, he drove. He was still drunk, that truck weaved from one side to the other. I prayed no car would come from the other side. Praise God, none did. Finally, we got to his house. His wife was sewing, she'd been taking in sewing to pay the bills. He said, "Shelby Jean, I'm saved!" She didn't even look up, said, "Is that right?" He called his little four-year old girl over to come to him, she was afraid of him. He took her in his arms, said, "Honey, you've got a new daddy!"

Today that man is always in the pew . . . [and the preacher's voice becomes thunderous again as he goes on to describe how the former reprobate is now a family man and an upstanding citizen].

Conversion is reported by *testimony*. The preceding account would qualify as testimony if it had been delivered by the person saved rather than by the preacher. At a service, the preacher may invite anyone who feels like it to testify. At Crusade Baptist Church, when the preacher offered this opportunity, right after the hymn singing, a man of about twenty-five distinguished from the rest of the congregation by his mod clothes, long sideburns, and mustache stood up in the back row and walked to the pulpit. He identified himself as employed at a hospital and, in an ungrammatical, possibly northern Appalachian accent, told his tale. He was a wild fellow, roaring around on his motorcycle until he had a wreck and had to lie in bed for three months unable to do anything except think about his life. During that time, he said, "God came into me." He went on to say that during his hospitalization, "I lost my wife, but I got God," and he says he's interested in finding another wife of a good, Christian type.

I do not have the data to demonstrate that the conversion experience leads to any enduring change in attitude and behavior, but the believers claim results. The convert is supposed to have new peace of mind, he stops drinking, whoring, and gambling, and he becomes a faithful churchgoer and a good family man. He becomes the type who stands up and is counted, who puts on his Sunday suit, helps take up collection, will pray publicly, and shakes hands with the visitor while looking him straight in the eye. In business, he is trustworthy and honest, or supposed to be, as Max Weber himself noted when he visited his cousin in the North Carolina mountains during the early twentieth century, and observed a man being baptized in order to assure his honesty as a banker (Weber 1946:304).

A very different conception of action guides the Muhammadijah of Indonesia. Some background first. Inspired by the reformist Islam of Muhammad Abduh of Cairo, the Muhammadijah was founded by K. H. A. Dahlan in Jogjakarta, Java in 1912. Muhammadijah is today the most powerful reformist movement of the Malayo-Indonesian region; it is still expanding, and it has hundreds of branches throughout the islands. It is an educational, social, and missionary organization. Its first duty is to institute pure Islam, as defined by the holy Qur'an, and to rid the islands of the Hinduist-Buddhist-animist magic and ritual that corrupt and contaminate. It has the most important private, non-Christian school, health, and welfare system in Indonesia and the most powerful Muslim women's organization in the world. Until it was banned by Sukarno, Masjumi, the political party with which Muhammadijah was affiliated, was one of the three most powerful in Indonesia. Originated by small merchants, Muhammadijah reflects bourgeois values, and it is strikingly parallel to the Calvinist-capitalist complex elaborated by Weber, though there are differences.[6]

The Muhammadijan equivalent to the Southern Baptist's Sunday church service is the Friday mosque service, which consists of ablutions, group chanting and praying, and a sermon (*chotbah*). The congregation in the main mosque of each community is basically male, though females are permitted to worship in smaller, separate mosques or in rear compartments and balconies. Entirely lacking from the Muhammadijan service is the invitation as well as the testimonial. Indeed, I could find no evidence of a Muhammadijan undergoing an emotional conversion experience, either as part of his joining the

Muhammadijan or shifting from another religion to Islam. These three elements, invitation, conversion, and testimonial, which are central to the religious action of the Southern Baptist, appear to be absent from that of the Muhammadijan.

To document this assertion, let me describe the closest equivalent to the testimonial that I could discover among the Muhammadijans. These were accounts of personal life and religious experience which each Muhammadijan was supposed to recount to his fellows during training camps designed to prepare him to better serve the organization. I shall summarize all the accounts narrated during an intensive fifteen-day training camp held in central Java by young leaders of rural branch organizations. During lulls in the daily eighteen-hour program of lectures, physical training, and discussion, the instructor would request each trainee to stand and give his personal introduction to his assembled fellows.

Trainee A begins by saying, "If you look at my age as revealed by gray hair you can see that I am about the same as Pak X [a popular leader within the group] for I have two such hairs." Following this humorous remark and laughter, he gives a brief sketch of his schooling and service to Muhammadijah. Participants then ask questions, such as why he has hesitated to marry, is he fearful of doing so? No questions were asked about his religious conviction.

B tells when he was born, apologizes that he had only an elementary school education, relates that he has worked in the governmental Department of Religion. He says his father and father-in-law are *modin* (which evokes laughter since these rustic muslim priests sometimes oppose Muhammadijah reformism).

C relates that he is head of Muhammadijah in a remote village, that he is a sawmiller. His wife is a graduate from the well-known Muhammadijah school Mualimaat, she is secretary of the women's movement, 'Aisjijah. He relates his own career in Muhammadijah, finally confesses, "To be frank, I just heard music that aroused my yearning for my wife and child, which is not fitting with the discipline of Muhammadijah."

D relates that he was born in the city of Semarang in 1933, he works in a government business which is soon to fail, so he will move into private enterprise. His wife was Christian, his father-in-law still is, his wife has now become head of the women's Muhammadijah movement. He has held various offices in Muhammadijah, he likes singing, and his one aim in life is that "each of his children become a protege of some prominent figure, for example Djarnawi [head of the national Muslim party] or Peacock."

E says that like many of village origins, he remembers the day and not the year of his birth. This is owing to the Hinduist-syncretist calendrical system, and he confirms that he was from a family of this syncretic persuasion which did not do the prayers of Islam. But he himself yearned to pray, and praise be to God, he is now a Muhammadijan (the group echoes, "Praise be to God.") He tells of helping to crush a mystical movement which "threatened the safety of society." Asked how many wives he has, he says, "One," and asked what his hobbies are, he says, "Badminton and *da'wah* [missionary activity]."

F tells when he was born and describes his wife's appearance and their marriage, his children. He says that he joined Muhammadijah in 1965, has since worked constantly at *da'wah,* and he used his army uniform to illegally wangle a free ticket here (laughter).

G tells of his education in both government and Muslim schools, his work as a trader, and that his wife is five years older than he. One of the participants asks how the marriage came about, and upon learning that his wife was active in the women's movement, further comments, "Because you are supported by your wife, you can truly do the movement, then when you are tired you can quickly fall asleep."

H states that he was born in 1929, had no training in religion, but his father was a leader of Muhammadijah, who "struggled" in that movement until he was arrested and disappeared. The informant, a lean, sinewy person who sometimes led us in the physical training exercises, tells of his experience in guerilla and paramilitary Muslim groups.

I tells of his education and work, then devotes most of his time to explaining that his wife is of Arab descent, that her family violently opposed their marriage, hence to this day the wife cannot return home.

In neither these nor similar accounts heard at other camps is there any mention of a conversion experience which led the participant to join Muhammadijah or Islam. Such experiences might have occurred (though other evidence suggests they do rarely if at all), but the reporting of conversion is not part of the Muhammadijan definition of public religious action, although it is part of the Baptist definition. The Muhammadijans emphasize their "struggle" (*perdjuangan*) for the movement *after* they join, rather than the experience of joining itself.

As I took part in such activities as these training camps, I was puzzled by what seemed to me a merely mechanical basis for the Muhammadijan's energetic and dedicated struggle to educate, preach, and reform. I kept seeking some deep emotional change, such as the conversion experience, which I felt was necessary to sustain such drive. Finding no such experience, I mentioned my bewilderment to some of the Muhammadijans. On two occasions I even discussed the matter with Muhammadijan study groups, one organized by the Young Muslim Intellectuals, and a second at the home of Professor Mukti Ali, who is now Minister of Religion for the Republic of Indonesia. These discussions suggest the following comparison between the conceptions of action of the Southern Baptists and the Muhammadijans.

Believing that he is born sinful or has sinned, the Baptist feels guilt which he absolves through the conversion experience when he accepts Jesus. The purity that he achieves through this conversion can be sustained only through rigid abstention from such pollutants as liquor and through a generally pious, upstanding demeanor.

The Muhammadijan does not, in the first place, believe in original sin, and Muhammadijans emphasize that they do not see as an important motivation of their action the desire to be saved from a state of sin. They emphasize instead that they should always sustain peace of mind, *ichlas,* through consistent conformity to the law set forth in the holy Qur'an. Among the laws which they derive from these scriptures is that of practicing pure Islam, and this necessitates constant reform of the syncretic magic that surrounds them. Reform derives essentially from the obligation to conform to the law.

In sum, Muhammadijans and Southern Baptists could be characterized in Weberian fashion as guided by contrasting paradigms of action: the dramatistic and the legalistic. The legalistic Muhammadijan sustains his reformist struggle in order to continuously conform to the laws of the scripture; his action is dictated directly by belief codified as law. The dramatistic Southern Baptist derives from his beliefs a torment that is resolved only through the conversion; his action stems from tension generated by belief rather than from conformity to belief instituted as law. The two faiths exemplify contrasting types of relationship between action and belief.

I would suggest these reasons for the contrasting paradigms.

1. Islam is generally more legalistic, Christianity more dramatistic. The Qur'an is essentially a collection of moral teachings and laws uttered by Allah through Muhammad, whereas the New Testament is, in the words of Frank Slaughter, "the greatest story every told," an account of the drama of Christ's birth, life, and death, and as a narrative model is more meaningful than any legal code for the Christian. A survey by me of four hundred Muhammadijans revealed that only 1 percent found the story of Muhammad's life or death emotionally meaningful to them, and a large minority found meaning only in his laws and precepts rather than in the story of his life; it is difficult to

imagine that the same results would be found concerning Christ for a comparable sample of Southern Baptists.

2. The educational process of the Muhammadijah leads toward gradually increasing knowledge of and conformity to the law; the boy progresses through different levels of qur'anic schooling, then following circumcision, into participation in the male congregation of the mosque. Through revivals, camp meetings, tent meetings, and the like, the Baptists have traditionally encouraged the sudden entry of those who make up for doctrinal ignorance by emotional conviction.

3. The Muhammadijan congregation is essentially male, that of the Southern Baptist is of mixed sex. Note that the whiskey maker, a reprobate, a man's man became, through conversion, domesticated. Ceasing to run around with the boys, he became part of a partially female congregation and began to stay home with his wife and daughter. Joining the all-male congregation of the mosque and Muslim community (*umat*), the Muhammadijan male is not domesticated or effeminized; in fact, his joining affirms his identity as a male, at least in terms of the machismo model of Islam. Because the Muhammadijan can join the congregation without sacrificing his masculinity, he can do so without undergoing the drastic (and in some ways emasculating)[7] conversion experience of the male Southern Baptist.

In conclusion, a word might be added concerning the Weberian methodology elucidated at the beginning of this paper. The Weberian way of *Verstehen* requires empathy between subject and analyst and thus resembles the phenomenological approach which has been heralded in Indonesian studies only recently (Lansing 1974) and I think, not yet in Southern studies. Yet the Weberian perspective differs from the phenomenological, as I understand it, in its impatience to go beyond contemplation of the process by which analyst relates to subject and to formulate an ideal type that highlights gross and distinctive features of the subject's characteristic mode of action. I consider my legalistic and dramatistic patterns as such ideal types, drawn from the particular data of Southern Protestantism and Indonesian Islam but more or less applicable in other contexts as well. In good Weberian spirit, these two types have use only insofar as they provide initial guidance to the phenomenologist who endeavors to probe the particularities of action and belief in Indonesia, the South, or elsewhere, and to the anthropologist who desires to correlate subjective orientations with such "objective" contexts as the social.

NOTES

I am grateful to the National Science Foundation, the American Council for Learned Societies, the Wenner-Gren Foundation for Anthropological Research, and the University of North Carolina for financial support of the Indonesian research from which data in this paper are drawn. I also wish to acknowledge the helpful comments of Carole Hill and Irma Honigmann.

[1]The best exposition of the Weberian theory of action and the Parsonsian elaboration of it, is in Parsons (1947, 1968) and Weber (1947, 1964).

[2]In light of Needham's (1972) recent demonstration that belief is not a universal category of experience, it should be noted that Weber's definition of action was not wedded specifically to belief, but simply to some type of subjective orientation.

[3]The best explanation of this scheme is Parsons (1947:14).

[4]This pattern is best described by Hill (1966) and was elaborated speculatively by Peacock (1971).

[5]"Quotations" of Southern Baptist and Muhammadijan utterances are not verbatim in that they were taken neither from tape-recordings nor on-the-spot notes (both of which seemed inappropriate for the circumstances) but from notes I wrote from memory shortly after hearing these utterances. And since the Muhammadijan utterances were in the Indonesian language, my notes translated these into English. In spite of the slippage that doubtless resulted through lack of note-taking and tape-recording and through translation, I believe I have retained accurately the main points and phrasing of crucial passages, though much interstitial detail is lost.

[6]The Muslim and Muhammadijan pattern is elaborated in Peacock (1973, ch. 4, 7).

[7]Note that the motorcycle rider was penetrated by God as he converted, a theme suggesting a regressive, homosexual dependency during the experience though not necessarily following it. The reader will observe that my data and interpretation concerning both Southern Baptist conversion experience and Muhammadijan lack of it pertain only to males; the question of why Southern Baptist females convert is beyond the scope of this paper.

REFERENCES

Hill, Samuel S., 1966. *Southern Churches in Crisis* (New York: Holt, Rinehart and Winston).

Lansing, Stephen, 1974. From *Umwelt* to *Lebenswelt*: The Application of Husserlian Models to Structural Anthropology. (Paper presented to the Conference on Symbolism in Indonesia, Malaysia, and the Phillipines, Ann Arbor, Michigan, April 26-27.)

Needham, Rodney, 1972. *Belief, Language, and Experience* (Chicago: University of Chicago Press).

Parsons, Talcott, 1947. Introduction. In *The Theory of Social and Economic Organization* by Max Weber, trans. A. M. Henderson and Talcott Parsons (Glencoe: Free Press), pp. 3-86.

————, 1968. *The Structure of Social Action: A Study in Social Theory with Special Reference to a Group of Recent European Writers* (New York: Free Press).

Peacock, James L. 1971. The Southern Protestant Ethic Disease. In *The Not So Solid South*, J. Kenneth Morland, ed., Southern Anthropological Society Proceedings, No. 4 (Athens: University of Georgia Press), pp. 108-113.

————, 1973. *Indonesia: An Anthropological Perspective* (Pacific Palisades, Cal.: Goodyear).

Samuelsson, Kurt, 1964. *Religion and Economic Action: A Critique of Max Weber,* trans. Geoffrey French (New York: Harper and Row).

Weber, Max, 1946. *From Max Weber: Essays in Sociology,* trans. and ed. H. H. Gerth and C. Wright Mills (New York: Oxford University Press).

————, 1947. *The Theory of Social and Economic Organization,* trans. and ed. Talcott Parsons and A. M. Henderson (New York: Oxford University Press).

————, 1951. *The Religion of China: Confucianism and Taoism,* trans. and ed. H. H. Gerth (Glencoe: Free Press).

————, 1958. *The Protestant Ethic and the Spirit of Capitalism,* trans. and ed. Talcott Parsons (New York: Scribners).

————, 1964. *The Sociology of Religion,* trans. E. Fischer (Boston: Beacon Press).

————, 1967a. *The Religion of India: The Sociology of Hinduism and Buddhism,* trans. and ed. H. H. Gerth and D. Martindale (Glencoe: Free Press).

————, 1967b. *Ancient Judaism,* trans. H. H. Gerth and D. Martindale (Glencoe: Free Press).

Vomiting for Purity: Ritual Emesis in the Aboriginal Southeastern United States

CHARLES HUDSON

ON certain occasions the Indians of the Southeastern United States deliberately induced vomiting. This practice also occurred elsewhere in the New World. The Aztecs and Incas made considerable use of emesis in therapeutic and ritual contexts (Ackerknecht 1949:636: de la Vega 1961:38-39). The Jivaro made an infusion from the leaves of *Ilex guayusa* which they drank in the morning to induce vomiting,[1] and several tribes in northern South America used herbal emetics (Cooper 1949:546-547). Several groups of Plains Indians induced vomiting at the conclusion of their Sun Dance ceremony (Merrill, personal communication). The Iroquois are reported to have used twelve or fourteen herbal emetics (Vogel 1970:174).

Many additional examples could be cited, but none appear to have vomited as enthusiastically as the Southeastern Indians. Although both sexes in the aboriginal Southeast resorted to it when they were diagnosed as having certain illnesses, its most characteristic use was by Southeastern Indian men, who vomited before hazardous or critical undertakings. Southeastern Indian men always vomited before going to and after returning from war; they always did it during their Green Corn ceremony (busk); they regularly did it before playing a game of stickball; and they sometimes did it before holding council. According to James Adair (1775:passim), who was a trader among the Cherokee and Chickasaw Indians from 1735 until 1768 and who knew them well, the men vomited in order to purify themselves. Indeed, the Southeastern Indians were so concerned with purity and pollution, with prohibitions and interdictions, with categorical tidiness and abominations, that Adair became convinced they were descended from the Lost Tribes of Israel.

The psychology and physiology of vomiting are well understood. Fundamentally, vomiting is a reflex which empties the upper gastrointestinal tract of its contents. The most common cause is an irritant in the gastrointestinal tract, particularly in the first portion of the duodenum, but irritation in the stomach and even in the pharynx can induce the reflex. It can also be triggered by psychological factors. Any sight, sound, or smell which causes an individual to feel nauseous can trigger the reflex. Finally, with practice people can learn to induce vomiting voluntarily, as evidenced by yoga adepts who do it by drinking a few glassfuls of water and by "churning" the stomach for a few minutes (Bernard 1972:37).

Just before the onset of vomiting the mouth fills with excessive quantities of saliva, and we shall presently see that this aspect of vomiting was of some importance to the Southeastern Indians. The first muscular movement is a strong contraction in the upper small intestine. This forces the contents of the upper jejunum, duodenum, and pyloric portion of the stomach into the fundus and the body of the stomach, which is relaxed and dilated. Then the esophagus relaxes, and after an inspiratory movement, the glottis closes and the abdominal muscles contract sharply. The pressure from this forces the gastric contents out through the esophagus (Best 1966:1220-1222).

The devices the Southeastern Indians used to induce vomiting are also well understood. They used virtually every device known to modern medicine. The simplest was to stick a finger, a blade of grass, or a feather down the throat (Mooney and Olbrechts 1932:23). But their most common way of inducing it was by drinking emetics made from various herbs. Lyda Averill Taylor (1940:72), in a survey of Southeastern herbal medicines, reports that the Southeastern Indians employed more herbal medicines to induce emesis than for any other medicinal use, and they used these herbs more effectively to achieve emesis than for any other use. The most frequently used herbal emetic in the Southeast was button snake-root (*Eryngium yuccifolium* Michaux), which has diuretic, expectorant, and diaphoretic properties, and is an emetic when taken in large doses (Taylor 1940:45-46). Perhaps of equal importance was bark from the roots of the willow tree, an astringent and an emetic (Taylor 1940:12). They also used as emetics rattlesnake fern (*Botrychium virginianum* Swartz), great bulrush (*Scirpus validus* Vahl), common rush (*Juncus effusus* Linnaeus), spicebush (*Lindera benzoin* Blume), white wild indigo (*Baptisia leucantha* Torrey & Gray), poison ivy (*Rhus toxicodendron* Linnaeus), blue flag (*Iris versicolor*), and boneset (*Eupatorium perfoliatum* Linnaeus). In some places the Southeastern Indians induced vomiting by drinking black drink or *cassina,* a tea made from the parched leaves and twigs of *Ilex vomitoria* Aiton, whose principal ingredient is caffeine. But here the picture is not clear, because they often drank black drink as a social beverage, much as we drink coffee or tea, with no vomiting (cf. Bartram 1958:284-286). Perhaps they used black drink to induce vomiting by suddenly drinking a large quantity of the hot liquid. Olbrechts reports that Cherokee medicine men routinely prescribed just as much medicine as a patient could hold—from two to seven liters a day—and in so doing they got emetic results from medicines which were not emetics (Mooney and Olbrechts 1932:56-57). Or perhaps because they vomited so frequently, to some degree they conditioned themselves to vomit, and this along with the hot black drink might have been sufficient to trigger the reflex. That they were able to exercise some control over vomiting is implied in the incident reported by Louis Le Clerc Milfort who lived among the Creeks in the late eighteenth century. Milfort (1972:91) tells of drinking black drink along with Alexander McGillivray and some Creek men of Coweta town. To his astonishment, the men began vomiting "easily and with no effort." When McGillivray asked him if he wished to vomit, he replied that he would let nature take its course, assuming that the black drink would do the work. But when McGillivray translated what he had said into Creek, there was a great burst of laughter.

What remains to be explained, particularly to those who, like myself, have always hated to vomit, is why they did it at all. The custom is still practiced to a limited extent by contemporary Southeastern Indians in Oklahoma, but they only retain vestiges of the old Southeastern belief system, and their explanation of why they practice the custom today would not be a reliable guide to aboriginal belief and practice. The only alternative, and the one to be taken here, is to try to answer the question historically. The most important single body of historical evidence is the Cherokee formulae which were written by medicine men in the Sequoyan syllabary and collected by James Mooney, Frans Olbrechts, Jack and Anna Kilpatrick, and others.

From historic sources one can glean enough information to reconstruct the major outlines of the belief system of the Southeastern Indians. It is far too complex to summarize here, but skeletally it consisted of a series of polar opposites (Hudson n.d.). The most fundamental was the opposition between the Upper World, which existed above the vault of the sky and was associated with continuity, order, and structure, and the Under World, which existed beneath the earth and the waters and was associated with disorder, fertility, madness, and change. The Southeastern Indians believed that they themselves lived in This World, between the Upper World and the Under World, trying to strike a balance as they lived out their lives.

The earthly representative of the Upper World was sacred fire, the ultimate symbol of purity and continence, which once burned perpetually in the temple of the Natchez Indians, and which other Southeastern Indians kindled on certain ritual occasions. The earthly representative of the Under World was the river, whom the Cherokees personified as the "Long Man," straining at its banks, always threatening to break out, symbolizing tumultuous life. The opposition between sacred fire and river water was directly expressed in the widespread interdiction in the Southeast that a fire was never to be extinguished by throwing water on it. Only on the occasion of a person's death would they sometimes thrust a firebrand into water, perhaps symbolizing the ultimate descent into cosmic disorder.

As in a number of cultures, the Cherokee microcosm was structurally similar to their macrocosm, such that saliva and vomitus were to the individual what the river was to the cosmos. This ideological linkage provides a clue to the meaning the Cherokees attached to vomiting. While we in our culture regard saliva as only marginally a part of our bodies, ranking perhaps a little higher than feces or urine, the Cherokees regarded it as centrally important in a person's being. Cherokee love formulae are often directed at several parts of the body and being of the one on whom the conjury is being worked. These parts include a person's soul, thoughts, song, flesh, breath, body, attire, heart, blood, and saliva (Kilpatrick and Kilpatrick 1965:45, 59, 62-68, 69-71, 114-115). Among these, saliva occupied a relatively important place. In Cherokee magical formulae the parts of a thing or the members of a series are generally uttered in order of importance, beginning with the lowest and ending with the highest. When saliva is a member of such a series, it is generally mentioned last (Kilpatrick and Kilpatrick 1965:115).

The Cherokees believed that a person's psychological and spiritual condition was intimately connected with his saliva. For example, in one of the love formulae collected by the Kilpatricks, a conjurer asks a great spiritual being to come and put spider saliva into his mouth. Because the spider is a creature of great cunning and stealth who leaps upon his prey and binds it up alive, this formula presumably enabled a person to bind up the soul of the object of his affections so that it would be his alone (Kilpatrick and Kilpatrick 1965:46-47). The Cherokees also believed that a person's saliva could become "spoiled," and when this happened he became despondent, withered away, and might even die. To dream of ghosts or of Under World animals, such as snakes or fish, could cause one's saliva to spoil. It could also be spoiled by the action of a witch, who was believed to be able to change the food in one's stomach, causing it to sprout or to change into organic matter and make one ill (Mooney and Olbrechts 1932: 280-281). James Mooney (1891:392) collected a conjurer's formula to cause a person to fall ill which required the conjurer to first collect a bit of his victim's spittle and then work his conjury on this spittle. In some places in the Southeast the Indians believed that witches did the nefarious things they did because their innards were filled with snakes and lizards; that is, their insides had been changed in a particularly terrible way.

Saliva linked a person's body and the outside world; it was, as it were, the road to a person's inner being. This explains the great ritual importance of food to the Southeastern Indians (Adair 1775: 133-134). The early French colonists along the lower Mississippi River reported that the Natchez would often refuse to eat French food because they feared it had not been prepared properly and was therefore impure (Swanton 1911:78). In the Cherokee myths collected by James Mooney, people often suffer terrible consequences from eating impure or improper foods. For example, in the story about the origin of bears, an entire clan of Cherokees was transformed into bears as a consequence of eating the wild foods of bears, the implication being that they were too lazy to produce and prepare the food appropriate to human beings (Mooney 1900:325-327). In other stories, people who go to visit the Under World and who are foolish enough to eat Under World food inevitably die after returning to This World. Moreover, this may explain why the aboriginal Southeastern Indians thoroughly cooked almost everything they ate (Adair 1775:135,412). They cooked their meat more thoroughly than did Europeans (Milfort 1972:74). They ate no raw salad vegetables and few uncooked vegetable foods except fruits and nuts (Adair 1775:412; Swanton 1911: 78). They believed that the food one ate had a profound effect on one's psychological, physical, and spiritual condition.

In light of these beliefs, vomiting was a logical course of action for anyone with an illness diagnosed as having anything to do with saliva or improper food or certain kinds of witchcraft. When one had such an illness, the Cherokee practice was to fast for a time, then to drink an emetic in one's home, and then to rush to the bank of a river. The best location for this was at the bend of a river where one could face east while looking upstream, and the best time was at dawn when the sun's rays began to reflect on the water. Here the person could vomit into the river so that the water would carry his illness away (Mooney and Olbrechts 1932:23, 63, 83). The Indians sometimes used this occasion for divination. If the vomitus floated it was a favorable sign, while if it sank it was an unfavorable sign.[2]

In addition to vomiting at a river bank, many of the magical

formulae were believed to be most efficacious when uttered at the
bank of a river or beside a flowing spring, facing east. A person
recited the formula while he rubbed water over his face or his body
(Kilpatrick and Kilpatrick 1965:89). In the event that a person could
not get to water, he could simply spit on his hands and rub the saliva
over his face or body (Kilpatrick and Kilpatrick 1965:80). Thus, saliva
was clearly equivalent to river or spring water.[3] Consistent with this
equivalence and with the Cherokee insistence on keeping the Upper
World and the Under World distinct, they had a rule against spitting
into a fire and against throwing anything with spittle on it into a
fire. Moreover, at least some evidence suggests that blood was to fire
what saliva was to river water—the microcosm replicated the macrocosm. For example, the Cherokees had a rule against women washing
the blood of game animals in the river, and apparently they had a
particularly stringent rule against putting menstrual blood into the
river (Mooney and Olbrechts 1932:38). On the other hand, it was
perfectly all right to put blood into a fire. Thus, a hunter was supposed to throw a small piece of the game he had killed, usually a
piece of the liver, into the fire as an offering. One is reminded of the
Yuchi origin myth, in which the Yuchi people originated from some
drops of blood which fell to earth from the sun during her menses
(Wagner 1931:147-150).

The polarity in Southeastern Indian thinking was symbolized in
the opposition of the colors red and white. Red was the color of
social divisiveness, white, the color of social cohesion. One is tempted
to conclude that in the Southeastern Indian belief system blood was
opposed to saliva as the color red was opposed to the color white.
Consistent with white being the color of peace and harmonious social
intercourse, the Cherokees thought of saliva as something which connected people together. For example, in a formula collected by the
Kilpatricks, the purpose of which was to attract a person of the opposite sex, the formula ends with the saliva of the two lovers joined
together never to be separated again (Kilpatrick and Kilpatrick 1965:
23-24). Consistent with this, in Cherokee myths and formulae, the
river, with its network of creeks and rivulets lacing the countryside, is
presented as a being which connects things one to another.

The Southeastern Indians appear to have seen some connection
between saliva and breath and perhaps speech as well. For example,
the Cherokees frequently worked their conjury by means of "remade
tobacco." A formula was ritually infused into some tobacco (*Nicotiana
rustica*) which was later smoked and the smoke blown in the direction
of the person being conjured, or else the tobacco was smoked in his

presence. One could chew the tobacco as well as smoke it. Thus, in a formula for retaining the affection of one's spouse or sweetheart, one waited until the person was asleep, uttered the formula, then chewed a piece of the tobacco and rubbed some of the tobacco spittle on the body of the loved one (Kilpatrick and Kilpatrick 1965:112-113). Or if one had no tobacco, one could simply blow one's breath or rub one's saliva onto his or her body. A connection between saliva and speech is also suggested by James Adair, who says somewhere that the Indians would often spit several times just before they asked for something. And John Swanton (1928:313) tells us that Creek orators would spit four times and utter a formula before delivering an oration.

It is far easier for us to understand why individual Southeastern Indians induced vomiting for one or another of their illnesses than why entire groups of men vomited to attain purity. As in other cultures, purity for the Southeastern Indians must be defined structurally, as a function of their concern with protecting the integrity of their categories of understanding (Douglas 1966). For the Southeastern Indians purity must have had meaning in terms of the values they attached to blood and saliva, the sun and the river, the Upper World and the Under World, and to other categories in their belief system. We may be sure that the increased salivation just before the onset of vomiting was symbolically important to them, and it seems that they thought of vomiting as a kind of salvation. They often fasted before vomiting, and this perhaps explains why some of the early historical accounts describe their vomitus as being clear (Lawson 1967:229). But beyond this it is difficult and perhaps impossible to be completely sure of what they believed they were doing when they vomited to attain purity. There are several possibilities.

One is that they may have vomited to prove they were pure. How else could one prove that one's saliva had not been changed, or that one had not eaten improper food? The Southeastern Indians believed that the success or failure of their undertakings, particularly their warfare, depended upon the strictness with which they observed interdictions on proper behavior and proper food (Adair 1775:380). It is conceivable that they would have wanted some proof of purity from every potential participant in a hazardous undertaking. This is what Louis Le Clerc Milfort thought their vomiting was for when he says, "The purpose of this disgusting ceremony is to assure the chief of the assembly that each of the members who compose it has a stomach free of food and consequently a clear head, and that all the deliberations will take place dispassionately; that strong liquors will not influence the decisions" (1972:92).

Another possibility is that they may have used vomiting for divination. It is amply documented that whenever the Southeastern Indians embarked on a raid or a game of stickball, they took divinatory readings at every step along the way. If an odd object floated into view when they went to the river for a ritual purpose, if a divinatory crystal gave off the wrong light, or if the wrong bird sang nearby, one member or even the entire group of men might return to their town without fear of being accused of cowardice. Hence, might they not have examined their vomitus just as they examined the contents of the river on ritual occasions?

One further possibility is that they may have thought of blood and saliva as existing in a balance with each other, so that in different situations they may have wanted the two components to exist in different proportions. Or perhaps the quantity or condition of blood and saliva varied independently of each other. In addition to vomiting, the Southeastern Indians also bled themselves on certain occasions. The usual way was to inflict a large number of light scratches on the arms, legs, and trunk using a comb-like instrument with sharp teeth. One rationale for ridding themselves of some blood was that too much blood made them heavy and sluggish. Hence, Cherokee men used to bleed themselves before playing the stickball game, which called for exceptional quickness and agility, as did aboriginal warfare.

I have saved until last the relatively easy explanations of medical materialism (Douglas 1966:29). Namely, their custom of vomiting and the value they attached to saliva may have entailed more than ideology or symbolism. For one thing, saliva is a sensitive litmus of one's social and psychological condition. Who has not had the experience of having a bad taste in the mouth when under social or psychological stress? And who has not had the experience of a dry mouth in such situations? But even though we know this to be true of saliva, these notions are only weakly codified in our folk knowledge. It shows up in one old Southern expression—I believe it occurs in some of the Uncle Remus stories—where one character speaks of giving another character the "dry grins," i.e., putting one's opponent in the position of knowing that he has most definitely been bested, but of still having to put on a brave front. But what we recognize only marginally, the Cherokees and probably other Southeastern Indians raised to a psychological and physiological principle.

A further possibility is that they may have gained some therapeutic advantage by vomiting. By vomiting they probably rid themselves of harmful gastrointestinal microorganisms or parasites. For example, the drug ipecac, derived from the bark of a tree (*Cephaelis ipecacuanha*) that grows in the Brazilian rain forest, is both an emetic and a laxative. The Brazilian Indians used it to treat amebic dysentery, and its alkaloid derivative, emetine, is used by modern doctors in exactly the same way (Vogel 1970:172-173).

   As in so many other detailed inquiries into the cultural and social life of the Southeastern Indians, this paper must end on an indefinite note. There is a point beyond which the historical record is mute. We can conclude that James Adair was right in interpreting the vomiting of the Southeastern Indians as a quest for purity. And we can go beyond Adair in interpreting the act of vomiting and the value and meaning of saliva in terms of the structure of their belief system. But we shall probably never be completely clear about whether they vomited to make themselves pure, to find out whether they were pure, or to foretell the future. To put it another way, did they believe that the fundamental purpose of vomiting was catharsis, diagnosis, or divination?

NOTES

I am grateful to the Institute for Behavioral Research at the University of Georgia for providing me with research time and the use of their facilities while this paper was being written. I am grateful to William Merrill, Rebecca Midgette, and Michael Olien for a number of valuable suggestions.
   [1]Like *Ilex paraguarensis,* from which Latin Americans make *maté,* and *Ilex vomitoria,* from which the Southeastern Indians made black drink, *Ilex guayusa* contains caffeine.
   [2]When Cherokee herbalists collected herbs they tied them into a bundle and put the bundle into a river or stream. If the bundle floated it was a sign that the herbs were efficacious. If it sank, they took this to be a sign that they were no good, and threw them away. In addition, they had several other techniques for divining in a stream of water.
   [3]During the Papago rain ceremony, the men drank large amounts of cactus beer to induce vomiting, the rationale being that just as they saturated themselves with liquor and regurgitated it onto the earth, so would clouds saturate the earth with rain (Merrill, personal communication).

REFERENCES

Ackerknecht, Erwin H., 1949. Medical Practices. In *Handbook of South American Indians,* vol. 5, Julian H. Steward ed., Bureau of American Enthnology Bulletin 143 (Washington, D.C.: Government Printing Office), pp. 621-643.
Adair, James, 1775. *The History of the American Indians* (London: Edward and Charles Dilly).
Bartram, William, 1958. *Travels of William Bartram,* Francis Harper, ed. (New Haven: Yale University Press).
Bernard, Theos, 1972. *Hatha Yoga: The Report of a Personal Experience* (New York: Samuel Weiser).
Best, Charles Herbert, 1966. *The Physiological Basis of Medical Practice* (Baltimore: Williams and Wilkins).
Cooper, John M., 1949. Stimulants and Narcotics. In *Handbook of South*

American Indians, vol. 5, Julian H. Steward, ed., Bureau of American Ethnology Bulletin 143 (Washington, D.C.: Government Printing Office), pp. 525-558.

de la Vega, Garcilaso, 1961. *The Incas,* trans. Maria Jolas (New York: Orion Press).

Douglas, Mary, 1966. *Purity and Danger: An Analysis of Concepts of Pollution and Taboo* (London: Routledge & Kegan Paul).

Hudson, Charles, n.d. The Southeastern Indians. (Manuscript.)

Kilpatrick, Jack F., and Anna G. Kilpatrick, 1965. *Walk in Your Soul: Love Incantations of the Oklahoma Cherokees* (Dallas: Southern Methodist University Press).

Lawson, John, 1967. *A New Voyage to Carolina* (Chapel Hill: University of North Carolina Press).

Milfort, Louis Le Clerc, 1972. *Memoirs, or a Quick Glance at My Various Travels and My Sojourn in the Creek Nation* (Savannah, Ga.: Beehive Press).

Mooney, James, 1891. *Sacred Formulas of the Cherokees.* In *Seventh Annual Report of the Bureau of American Ethnology* (Washington, D.C.: Government Printing Office), pp. 301-397.

––––––, 1900. *Myths of the Cherokee.* In *Nineteenth Annual Report of the Bureau of American Ethnology* (Washington, D.C.: Government Printing Office), pt. 1.

Mooney, James, and Frans Olbrechts, 1932. *The Swimmer Manuscript: Cherokee Sacred Formulas and Medicinal Prescriptions,* Bureau of American Ethnology Bulletin 99 (Washington, D.C.: Government Printing Office).

Swanton, John, 1911. *Indian Tribes of the Lower Mississippi Valley and Adjacent Coast of the Gulf of Mexico,* Bureau of American Ethnology Bulletin 43 (Washington, D.C.: Government Printing Office).

––––––, 1928. *Social Organization and Social Usages of the Indians of the Creek Confederacy.* In *Forty-second Annual Report of the Bureau of American Ethnology* (Washington, D.C.: Government Printing Office), pp. 23-472.

Taylor, Lyda Averill, 1940. *Plants Used as Curatives by Certain Southeastern Tribes* (Cambridge, Mass.: Botanical Museum of Harvard University).

Vogel, Virgil J. 1970. *American Indian Medicine* (Norman: University of Oklahoma Press).

Wagner, Günter, 1931. *Yuchi Tales,* Publications of the American Ethnological Society, vol. 13 (New York: G. E. Stechert).

Ethnometaphysics of Iroquois Ritual

Elisabeth Tooker

In *Primitive Culture,* Edward B. Tylor (1958:448-449) wrote, "In the science of religion, the study of ceremony has its strong and weak sides. On the one hand, it is generally easier to obtain accurate accounts of ceremonies by eyewitnesses, than anything like trustworthy and intelligible statements of doctrine. . . . On the other hand, the signification of ceremonies is not to be rashly decided on by mere inspection." Since Tylor's pioneering study in the anthropology of religion, ceremonials have continued to be described in the ethnographic literature, and anthropologists have continued to seek the meaning ("signification") of these rituals, if not always in history as Tylor did, in such areas as psychological and social process and function. In the last several decades, an increasing number of studies of symbolism have also appeared, and the disparity noted by Geertz (1966:42) between the number of studies analyzing "the system of meanings embodied in the symbols which make up the religion proper" and those relating "these systems to social-structural and psychological processes" seems to be rapidly closing.

Few recent studies, however, have either described or analyzed ritual form—the cultural patterns that underlie and govern the performance of religious ceremonies, or what might be called the structure of ritual, although the term *structure* has come to have certain other connotations. Yet, as various students of ritualism (for example, Kluckhohn and Wyman 1940 and Fenton 1936) have observed, the ceremonials that constitute the practice of a religion are not a haphazardly arranged collection of miscellaneous actions. Rather, like other parts of culture including language, religious practice has form and structure. As a language is not composed of an infinite number of words, so also a religion does not employ a limitless number of rites but a relative few, selecting and arranging them in accordance with customary rules to craft a specific ceremony much as words are combined into longer units of discourse in accordance with customary grammatical rules.

Part of the reason for the paucity of studies of ritual form may well be the largely unconscious nature of such patterns. As Sapir (1949b:549) noted,

> It is strange how frequently one has the illusion of free knowledge, in light of which one may manipulate conduct at will, only to discover in the test that one is being impelled by strict loyalty to forms of behavior that one can feel with the utmost nicety but can state only in the vaguest and most approximate fashion. It would seem that we act all the more securely for our unawareness of the patterns that control us.

And so at times the effort required to ascertain these forms may be considerable.

Nevertheless, the reward for such effort may be of equal magnitude—for if "Concealed in the structure of each different language are a whole set of assumptions about the world and life in it" (Kluckhohn 1949:159), so also a comparable set of assumptions may be concealed in the structure of ritual, in the patterns of religious behavior. Although to some the study of ritual form has seemed dry and dehumanizing, it does not necessarily have these consequences. Rather, studies as these may be of help in understanding such matters as belief, and more generally further the study of what Hallowell (1960:20) has termed "ethnometaphysics," and so, as Whorf (1956:218-219) said of the study of linguistic forms, make a significant contribution to the "greater development of our sense of perspective," indicating

> that the few thousand years of history covered by our written records are no more than the thickness of a pencil mark on the scale that measures our past experience on this planet; . . . that the race has taken no sudden spurt, achieved no commanding synthesis during recent millenniums, but has only played a little with a few of the linguistic formulations and views of nature bequeathed from an inexpressibly longer past. Yet . . . this . . . need [not] be discouraging to science but should, rather, foster that humility which accompanies the true scientific spirit, and thus forbid that arrogance of the mind which hinders real scientific curiosity and detachment.

But even if the study of ritual form should prove not to contribute to the discernment of the signification of ceremonies by indicating what the people themselves regard as important and what they feel can be properly ignored, what things they deem to belong together and thus consider different in some manner from things not so classed, it may be of aid in the task of describing ritual practice. Attention to these forms suggests that eyewitness accounts may not be quite as trustworthy or accurate as Tylor implied, but often are distorted in much the same manner as early grammatical studies of non-Indo-European languages, based as they were on the model of Latin grammar.

At least it is the intent of the following discussion to suggest how studies of ritual form may contribute to our understanding of religion and, more tentatively, to our understanding of the mode of apprehension, the conception of the world, held by those who practice them. The example to be used is that of Iroquois ritualism, one of the best described in the ethnographic literature (Morgan 1851; Fenton 1936, 1941, 1953; Speck 1949; Shimony 1961; Tooker 1970).

Although a number of Iroquois now living in the state of New York and the provinces of Ontario and Quebec are Christians, not all are, and the traditional Iroquois religious ceremonies continue to be held in the Longhouses[1] (the "churches" of this religion) and in the homes of believers. The religion itself is sometimes called the "Longhouse religion" and those who practice it are sometimes referred to as the "Longhouse gang." And, although the Longhouse religion probably is not identical in every detail to the religion practiced in pre-Columbian times by the Iroquois, it undoubtedly derives from this practice, and in large part was affirmed by the Seneca prophet, Handsome Lake, who preached from 1799 to his death in 1815.

But if this religion is one of the best described in the ethnographic literature—for as Oswalt (1973:446) observes, "Anthropologists long have exhibited a particular fondness for the Iroquois"—consulting this literature can also be, as he says, "a frustrating experience." Like others, Oswalt (1973:447) suggests that what is needed is a synthesis of the ethnographic and ethnohistorical work on the Iroquois. However, not even such a compendium is likely to dispel completely suspicions similar to those Aberle (1963:1) has noted of anthropological studies of Navajo social organization, either that there is a certain "fuzzy" quality about this culture or that the fieldwork has been "sloppy." Furthermore, the nature of Iroquois ritual is such that certain types of analyses often regarded as being capable of providing more accurate, complete, and clearer descriptions prove difficult to do. For example, the student of Iroquois religious practice is not confronted with a wealth of data on certain matters frequently discussed in the study of religion.

The Longhouse itself, sometimes called a "council house" in Reservation English, is as starkly utilitarian as a Quaker meeting house. Typically, it is rectangular in plan, furnished only with benches along the walls and a fireplace or stove at either end. There is no altar, nor are altars built as part of a ceremony. No sacred objects are kept in the Longhouse, and in fact such objects and other visual symbols figure little in the ritual as do formalistic prayers and stylized gestures. Rather the ritual consists of speeches, songs, dances, and games—many of which may also be performed on secular occasions. Only a tenuous connection exists between ritual performance and myth; ceremonies do not enact myths, nor are myths concerned with the justification of the rituals.

Even the seemingly simple task of classifying Iroquois ceremonials is not without its difficulties. At first glance, these ceremonies would seem to be conveniently grouped under several headings, the four most important being the calendric agricultural ceremonies, the curing rituals of the medicine societies, the rites in which the teachings of the prophet Handsome Lake are recited, and the rites of passage.[2] But, although convenient, such a typology has its awkward features. As the following examples illustrate, sometimes a category includes rituals of a kind not indicated by its descriptive label and sometimes the classification omits rituals that have a place in the religion.

Not all the so-called agricultural ceremonies are, in fact, concerned with agriculture. Often listed in the agricultural series (the series is not identical in all Longhouses) are the Midwinter ceremony (held in January or February), the Maple ceremony (March or April), the Planting ceremony (May), the Strawberry ceremony (May or June), the Green Bean ceremony (August), the Green Corn ceremony (August or September), and the Harvest ceremony (October or November). However, some examination of ritual form indicates that the Maple and Strawberry ceremonies are not properly agricultural ones, Maple more obviously and Strawberry less obviously so. In Iroquois practice, the other five of this series (Midwinter, Planting, Green Bean, Green Corn; and Harvest) include as a major ritual a series of dances (the particular dances vary from Longhouse to Longhouse) called "Our Life Supporter" dances, and are dances for the three principal cultivated plants of the old Iroquois agriculture: corn, beans, and squash. The Our Life Supporter dances are not performed as part of the Strawberry ceremony; aboriginally, strawberries were not cultivated. Neither are they performed as part of the Maple ceremony, but the distinction made by the Iroquois is not between wild and cultivated plants; the principal rites of the Maple differ from those of the Strawberry ceremony.

As all these ceremonies involve foods used by the Iroquois, they might be termed "ceremonies addressed to food spirits" (cf. Speck 1949:37). However, this classification ignores such apparently agricultural-calendric rituals as the Sun, Moon, and Thunder ceremonies. Although in some Longhouses the Sun and Moon ceremonies are held only occasionally or not at all, in others they are performed each year as part of the ceremonial calendar. Similarly, in some Longhouses the Thunder ceremony may be performed in order to bring rain, and in some it is given each spring as a standard part of the calendric cycle.

A distinction between calendric and curing ceremonies as well as

Titiev's (1960) somewhat comparable distinction between "calendrical" and "critical" rites also poorly fit the Iroquois data. As has been noted, not all seemingly calendric ceremonies are always part of the ceremonial calendar. Conversely, a few ceremonies of the medicine societies are calendric. These include certain rites of the Little Water and the False Face societies, as well as the rites various medicine societies perform during the most important calendric observance, the Midwinter ceremonial. Furthermore, rituals other than those of the medicine societies may be used to cure illness. Virtually any ritual may be performed (if indicated) to cure a sick individual, including those most commonly performed as part of a calendric ceremony.

Such inadequacies as these may seem trival compared to the impressive accomplishment of these classifications—that of conveying in a limited number of pages the content of a complex religious system. Yet, the seemingly trivial inadequacies of such typologies may also indicate that the principles used in other cultures are different from those in common use in ours. Thus, some study of the structure of culture, those forms which "establish a definite relational feeling or attitude . . . towards all possible contents of experience" (Sapir 1949a: 153) may aid in ascertaining these principles and dispel the idea that there is a fuzzy quality about some cultures.

Although it would be rash to claim that, given the present state of knowledge, anything more than a most tentative characterization of the principles governing Iroquois ritual performance can be given, some inspection of the data suggests that the Iroquois pay particular attention to what may be called "appearance," and more specifically to such matters as where things and beings are located, with whom or to whom or with what they appear, and changes in their appearance. Further study may prove that the underlying structure and categories of Iroquois ritual in particular and Iroquois culture in general are much like those of Western civilization. But contrary to some assertions, a basic universal structure (if it does exist) is little understood, and before it is properly known, more extensive analysis of its variant expressions in different cultures than has been made to date may well be necessary. Perhaps, then, the following outline—tentative as it necessarily is—of the principles governing the how, when, where, and who of Iroquois rtiualism ultimately may contribute to such an understanding.

PRINCIPLES GOVERNING THE "HOW" OF
IROQUOIS CEREMONIAL PRACTICE

The basic framework of an Iroquois ceremony consists of five parts: Thanksgiving Speech, tobacco invocation, rites and/or speeches,[3] brief Thanksgiving Speech, and distribution of food. Each of these parts may or may not be included in a specific ceremony according to the following rules.

Rule 1. Most ceremonies, or more properly most gatherings (little or no distinction is made between the secular and sacred, the natural and supernatural worlds, and religious ceremonies and ordinary meetings generally have the same form) begin with the Thanksgiving Speech. The principle exception to this rule are various ceremonies for the dead; it would be inappropriate to be thankful for death (Chafe 1961:2).

Although the Iroquois word for this address is usually translated "Thanksgiving Speech," more is implied than just the idea of thanking. As Chafe (1961:1) has noted, "The trouble is that the Seneca concept [of thanksgiving] is broader than that expressed by any simple English term, and covers not only the conventionalized amenities of both thanking and greeting, but also a more general feeling of happiness over the existence of something or someone." There is, then, an element of greeting, and more particularly "greeting" as expressing happiness for the existence of a being or thing in the Iroquois notion of thanksgiving. For this reason, in part, the Thanksgiving Speech begins most ceremonies. The speech greets and "returns thanks to"— to use the Reservation English expression—various beings and things.

The burden of the Thanksgiving Speech is the mention of the various items found on the earth and above. In the long versions (different speakers use slightly different versions and the length of the speech may vary), sixteen such items often are mentioned specifically: the people, the earth, the plants (including special mention of the strawberry), the water, the trees (including special mention of the maple), the animals, the birds, the Three Sisters (Our Life Supporters—corn, beans, and squash), the wind, the Thunderers, the sun, the moon, the stars, the Four Beings (messengers from the Creator who appeared to Handsome Lake), Handsome Lake, and the Creator. In the section of the Thanksgiving Speech devoted to each of these items, mention is made first that the Creator decided on, and so ordained the existence of the item. Next the item is described, and mention is made that it is still present and carrying out the responsibility assigned to it. Finally, thanks are returned for it (Chafe 1961:7). Although various speakers mention the items in a slightly different order, all follow the same general order: the items "below" (those on earth) are mentioned first, then the items "above," and within these categories the order is generally from the things nearest the earth upward to the things above.

Rule 2. In some ceremonies there follows after the Thanksgiving Speech a tobacco invocation, a speech during which a speaker throws loose tobacco into a fire. A tobacco invocation is given as part of the Maple ceremony, the Thunder ceremony, the ceremonies of the medicine societies, and certain ceremonies for the dead. It is not included in the Planting, Green Bean, Green Corn, Harvest, and other ceremonies involving the Our Life Supporters, the Strawberry ceremony, or, in some Longhouses, the Sun and Moon ceremonies.

The general rule suggested by these practices is: A tobacco invocation forms part of the ritual of those ceremonies for beings or things usually found at a distance (that is, beyond the village and its nearby fields), but not those for beings or things nearby. For example, the tutelaries of the medicine societies, such as the False Faces, live in the woods beyond the village and its fields, and a tobacco invocation forms part of the ritual of these societies. The maple trees grow in the forest, and a tobacco invocation forms part of the Maple ceremony. The Thunderers are heard beginning in the spring, but not in the winter—they are not always nearby, and a tobacco invocation is given in the Thunder ceremony. However, the Three Sisters (corn, beans, and squash) and strawberries grow nearby, and a tobacco invocation is not included in the ceremonies honoring them. A tobacco invocation is given if the dead are being addressed collectively or if a deceased person is being asked not to bother a sick individual (that is, make him ill), but not during the funeral ceremonies, those ceremonies for the dead held before the ghost has left for the land in the west.

This rule seems to rest on a basic and pervasive distinction made by the Iroquois between the world of the forest and that of the clearing. To the Iroquois, the forest was the domain of men. Men cut the clearing out of the forest for the fields and the village, building the houses and, if necessary, the stockade surrounding them out of materials of the forest. Once this was done the clearing became the domain of the women in particular and of the people generally.[4] Women spent much of their time in the village and the fields, doing almost all of the planting, tending, and harvesting of the crops, while the men were often away, hunting, trading, and warring. As a consequence, women dominated life in the village, men that beyond the clearing.

Rule 3. Speeches and/or rites appropriate to the occasion follow the Thanksgiving Speech and, if given, the tobacco invocation. If the gathering is held primarily for the purpose of reminding people or deciding what they should do, speeches follow. Speeches customarily are important in the following types of gatherings: If the primary intent is to remind people what a person or persons now dead (as the prophet Handsome Lake or the founders of the League of the Iroquois) said and did, the content of the speeches, although varying somewhat according to the knowledge of the speaker, is fixed by tradition. If the gathering is being held for the purpose of telling someone now deceased what he should do (for example, to tell him to stop making another ill), a speech is addressed to him. If it concerns deciding the responsibilities of people now living (such as matters of the kind discussed at ordinary council meetings), speeches also are given.

However, if the gathering is in recognition of one of the items mentioned in the Thanksgiving Speech, there follow rites drawn from the Iroquois repertoire of songs, dances, and games. The repertoire includes such songs as the Personal Chants; dances such as the Feather Dance, Thanksgiving (Skin or Drum) Dance, War Dance, Corn Dance, Stomp Dance, and those of the type known as social dances; and such games as the Bowl (Peach Stone) Game, lacrosse, and tug of war. In a ceremony given for an individual (for example, to restore or maintain health or other good fortune), the song, dance, or game (or some combination of such rites—more than one may be deemed necessary) is indicated in a dream of the individual concerned or suggested as appropriate by another. If the ceremony is for one of the other items mentioned in the Thanksgiving Speech, the choice from the repertoire of songs, dances, and games is fixed by tradition, a choice perhaps first dictated in a dream.

If the gathering involves items not mentioned in the Thanksgiving Speech (such as the tutelaries of the medicine societies), the rites performed are those songs and dances known only to a segment of the community. Individuals with such knowledge include members of the medicine society and often a few who are not members of the society; participation in such a ceremony is not necessarily restricted to those who belong to the society.

Rule 4. If the Thanksgiving Speech has been given at the beginning of the ceremony, there follows next an abbreviated Thanksgiving Speech.

Rule 5. Food is distributed at the conclusion of all gatherings except those which involve neither those beings or things found beyond the clearing nor those individuals living beyond it. For example, food is distributed at the end of (or forms part of) the medicine society rituals. Food is also distributed at the conclusion of such ceremonies as Maple, Planting, Strawberry, Green Bean, and Harvest and at the conclusion of each day's rituals in such ceremonials as Midwinter and

Green Corn that last more than one day. It is not distributed at the end of an evening of social dances in the Longhouse (often an evening social dance is held in the Longhouse if the ceremonial is to continue there the next day), but it is served when people from other reservations have been invited to the affair (for example, to a meeting of the singing societies from various reservations).

PRINCIPLES GOVERNING THE "WHEN" OF CEREMONIAL PRACTICE

Consistent with the general idea of greeting expressed in the Thanksgiving Speech, ceremonials and other gatherings are apt to be held when something or some persons "arrive," "appear," or at least change in appearance, or even when it is wished something (such as rain) will appear. In instances involving only people (for example, council meetings), gatherings are held when an individual or individuals request such a meeting, that is, wish to meet with (appear with or before) others.

If the ritual is for one of the items mentioned in the Thanksgiving Speech, the ceremony itself recognizes a change in appearance, and is so timed. For example, the Maple ceremony is held when the sap begins to flow in the maple trees, the Strawberry ceremony "when the berries hang on the bushes," the Thunder ceremony when the Thunderers are first heard in the west in the spring or when it is wished that thunder will be heard and rain fall, the Sun ceremony when the sun begins to feel warm in the spring, the Green Bean ceremony when the green beans are mature, and the Green Corn ceremony when the first corn is ripe. These ceremonies and others of this type are calendric only in the sense that the changes recognized occur at a certain time of the year and not in the sense that they are set in accordance with a fixed division of the year into arbitrary segments. In fact, the date on which a particular ceremony is to be held usually is known only a week or two in advance.[5]

The importance of the dream in determining what should be done to cure a sick person and consequently when curing rituals should be given also seems to be part of the general Iroquois concern with appearance. To the Iroquois, the dream indicates what should be done to maintain or obtain good fortune in general, and so maintain or restore good health. If an ill individual has not had a dream indicating what should be done to effect a cure, another, sometimes termed a "fortuneteller" (Shimony 1961:270), is consulted. Such a person ascertains the cure, employing one or more of a number of techniques including dreaming, looking into a bowl of water, formerly looking at a robe or skin or into a fire, and more recently looking at tea

leaves or cards. In general, then, both the type of cure and the necessity for it are indicated by an appearance of something to someone,
often but not always in a dream.

PRINCIPLES GOVERNING THE "WHERE" OF CEREMONIAL PRACTICE

Gatherings, including ceremonials, open to all are held in the
Longhouse and ceremonies open only to those who have been invited
are held in private houses.[6] The major exception to this principle are
ceremonies held in the so-called "closed" Longhouses, that is, those
Longhouses closed to whites and sometimes also Christian Indians.
However, this practice seems to be a relatively recent innovation,
instituted in part to keep out the merely curious. In other Longhouses,
no such rule presently obtains and the merely curious are kept away
by the simple but effective device of not widely advertising the date of
an upcoming ceremony.

In general, then, the place the ceremonial or other gathering is held
is correlated with who may properly attend or come, that is, who may
"appear." The medicine societies are not so much "secret" societies
as they have sometimes been termed (Parker 1909) as they are groups
performing rituals usually open only to those invited. The so-called
calendric ceremonies held in the Longhouse are not so much for
the community (or for members of a sect—if the Longhouse may be
termed such) as they are for the people generally, and consequently
whoever wishes may attend.

PRINCIPLES GOVERNING THE "WHO" OF CEREMONIAL PRACTICE

A concern with appearance is also evident in the selection of those
items mentioned in the ubiquitous Thanksgiving Speech. Included in
this speech are some items we would classify as supernatural beings
(for example, the Creator and the Four Beings), and others as
belonging to the natural world including animate (people, animals,
birds, plants, and trees) and inanimate things (earth, water, sun,
moon, and stars) as well as natural phenomena (wind and thunder).
But mentioning these diverse items together and treating them similarly
in the Thanksgiving Speech (the section of the Thanksgiving Speech
devoted to each follows the same form) suggests that to the Iroquois
they all belong to the same class, that they all share some common
characteristic. This characteristic may involve appearance: all are
items whose appearance may change. Some (such as sun, moon, and
animals) appear at different places at different times and others (such
as plants, trees, and water) change their appearance at different times.

Thus, they may not be so much "spirit forces," as some (Speck 1949 and Fenton 1936) have termed them, as "appearances."

Somewhat similarly the tutelaries of the medicine societies are known from having been seen. For example, the False Faces are known from having been seen in a dream or in the forest. But these tutelaries have not appeared to all, and hence are not mentioned in the Thanksgiving Speech.

Who participates in the rituals and consequently where the ceremony is held also may well rest on the characteristic of appearance. Anyone (with the exceptions noted above) may participate in the ceremonies held in the Longhouse, and generally these ceremonials are for those appearances known to all. Participation in the rituals of a medicine society is largely limited to those who "belong" to the society, that is, to those who have been cured by the society, and each society generally holds its ceremony in a private house.

More generally, group affiliation in Iroquois society seems to rest on the quality of appearance together. Most Iroquois groups, including religious ones, exhibit few if any of the features usually regarded as characteristic of corporate groups. They are not so much closed, property-holding units as they are collections of individuals who are apt to interact with each other, to be seen together on certain occasions. For example, one cannot join the Longhouse as one might join a Christian church, and the Longhouse does not own ritual or other intangible property. It is the kind of group quite accurately termed a "gang" in the Reservation English expression "Longhouse gang." Somewhat similarly, a medicine society is a group whose members have participated in the important rituals known to that society, that is, have been patients of and have been cured by the society.

In summary, then, I would suggest that the Iroquois are not the innocents portrayed by Alexander Pope in the lines:

Lo, the poor Indian; whose untutor'd mind
Sees God in clouds, or hears him in the wind;[7]

but rather, as Frank Cushing (1896:376) said of the Zuni, "theirs is a science of appearances and a philosophy of analogies."

All people, of course, must to a certain extent judge the nature of things on the basis of appearance. What may distinguish the Iroquois and perhaps also some other people is their attention to particular aspects of appearance that are of little consequence in Western society. At least I believe there is evidence for this in Iroquois religious practice. Ceremonials are held to greet the appearance of things or beings or a change in their appearance, and the things and beings so recognized are those that may change in appearance or may appear in different locations. The consideration of who may appear determines where a particular ceremony is held, and the appearance of the item being recognized by the ceremony dictates what rites are included in it. Even social groups are apt to be defined on the basis of appearance: that of being often seen together.

This attention to appearance may well be grounded in the economy once practiced by the Iroquois. Until the last century, the Iroquois practiced a mixed economy based on horticulture, fishing, hunting, and gathering—activities that required little ownership of land resources or means of production. Crucial for success in obtaining a livelihood probably was not control over property but knowledge of appearance. To be a successful hunter, one must pay attention to the appearance of the environment to know where the animals are. To be a successful fisherman, one must know when and where the fish will appear and how they appear in the waters. To be a successful gatherer of wild plants, one must know when they appear and which ones are useful to man—again to recognize appearance. And, as the Iroquois practiced slash-and-burn agriculture, what land might be cultivated may also have been recognized by its location and appearance.

To an extent, the Iroquois still find that attention to appearance is helpful in gaining a livelihood. Economic opportunities on the reservations are few, and the Iroquois who live on them often must "hunt" for jobs elsewhere. In this search, some find the old Iroquois assumptions about the world and life in it still useful, and as long as they do, the religion of the Longhouse may well continue also.

NOTES

[1]There are eleven Longhouses located on various Iroquois reservations in New York and Canada. Three were established in this century: the Oneida Longhouse on the Oneida Reserve in Ontario, the Caughnawauga Longhouse on the Caughnawauga Reserve near Montreal, and the St. Regis Longhouse on the St. Regis Reserve situated on both sides of the Canadian-United States border. Three are located in western New York State: the Coldspring Longhouse on the Allegany Reservation, the Newtown Longhouse on the Cattaraugus Reservation, and the Tonawanda Longhouse on the Tonawanda Reservation. A seventh, the Onondaga Longhouse is located on the Onondaga Reservation south of Syracuse in central New York State. The other four are located on the large Six Nations Reserve in Ontario: the Onondaga, Seneca, Lower Cayuga, and Sour Springs (Upper Cayuga) Longhouses.

[2]Although not all published accounts of Iroquois religion have used precisely this classification, something similar to it is evident in many of them, for example, in those by Shimony (1961), Speck (1949:37-38), and Wallace 1966:75-80).

[3]In Iroquois culture, there seems to be a category of actions that includes speeches, songs, dances, and games which has no exact equivalent in ours. In Reservation English, reference to such activities is included in the word *doings.* For example, instead of saying, "I am going to the ceremony," an Iroquois is apt to say, "I am going to the doings." In a sense, the main events at such gatherings include one or more particular "doings" drawn from the total body of speeches, dances, songs, and games. The scope of the discussion here precludes consideration of certain combinations of doings, such as those combining speeches and dances. However, these practices are not inconsistent with the outline given. For example, the Feather Dance that follows each day's recitation of the Code of Handsome Lake during the Six Nations meetings recognizes the role of the Creator in these teachings: that through His messengers, the Creator told Handsome Lake what He wanted the Iroquois to do. Also precluded is discussion of the brief speeches announcing the dance, song, or game that precedes its performance, of dances as the Thanksgiving Dance which are part speech, and other comparable combinations.

[4]In the Iroquoian languages, the feminine gender is used as the generic for "mankind" rather than the masculine as in English. Thus, in Iroquoian pairs comparable to the English "man/woman," "woman" is the unmarked member and refers either to female human beings or to people generally.

[5]This practice gives some further evidence that Titiev's distinction between "calendrical" and "critical" ceremonies poorly fits the Iroquois data. Titiev (1960:293) states that "Because of their very nature calendrical rituals can always be scheduled and announced long in advance of their occurrence." The timing of Iroquois ceremonies suggests that most could equally well be classified as "critical" ones, ceremonies of the type Titiev (1960:294) regards as being "designed to meet the pressing needs of a given moment" and so "never . . . announced, scheduled, or prepared for far in advance" although they "may be designed to benefit . . . a whole society, a relatively small group, or even a single individual."

Calendrical ceremonies (that is, ceremonies based on a true calendar) may be more common among those peoples having a division of labor that organizes society into functional groups, and so have what Durkheim (1933) called "organic solidarity." In Iroquois society, social solidarity seems to rest largely on similarities between individuals, not differences, and so on what Durkheim termed "mechanical" rather than organic solidarity. It may be that in societies with little organic solidarity, ceremonies usually are held in response to a situation known to all, rather than on an arbitrary date, set without regard to the wants and needs of individuals—a feature Titiev (1960:294) suggests means that calendrical ceremonies "can be interpreted only as having value for an entire society."

[6]I became aware of this principle when a Seneca told me of a couple who wished to be married in the Longhouse (a relatively infrequently performed ritual that seems to have developed relatively recently in response to white emphasis on their own forms of legal marriage) and to have only invited guests there (in obvious emulation of common practice among whites). They were told that if they wished to have the ceremony in the Longhouse, they could not limit attendance to those receiving invitations because the Longhouse was open to all.

[7]*An Essay on Man* (1733), Epistle I, ll. 99-100.

REFERENCES

Aberle, David F., 1963. Some Sources of Flexibility in Navaho Social Organization. *Southwestern Journal of Anthropology* 19:1-8.

Chafe, Wallace L., 1961. *Seneca Thanksgiving Rituals,* Bureau of American Ethnology Bulletin 183 (Washington, D.C.: Government Printing Office).

Cushing, Frank Hamilton, 1896. *Outlines of Zuni Creation Myths.* In *Thirteenth Annual Report of the Bureau of American Ethnology* (Washington, D.C.: Government Printing Office), pp. 321-447.

Durkheim, Emile, 1933. *The Division of Labor in Society,* trans. George Simpson (Glencoe: Free Press).

Fenton, William N., 1936. *An Outline of Seneca Ceremonies at Coldspring Longhouse,* Yale University Publications in Anthropology 9 (New Haven: Yale University Press).

----------, 1941. *Tonawanda Longhouse Ceremonies: Ninety Years after Lewis Henry Morgan,* Bureau of American Ethnology Bulletin 128 (Washington, D.C.: Government Printing Office).

----------, 1953. *The Iroquois Eagle Dance: An Offshoot of the Calumet Dance,* Bureau of American Ethnology Bulletin 156 (Washington, D.C.: Government Printing Office).

Geertz, Clifford, 1966. Religion as a Cultural System. In *Anthropological Approaches to the Study of Religion,* Michael Banton, ed., Association of Social Anthropologists Monographs No. 3 (London: Tavistock Publications), pp. 1-46.

Hallowell, A. Irving, 1960. Ojibwa Ontology, Behavior, and World View. In *Culture in History: Essays in Honor of Paul Radin,* Stanley Diamond, ed. (New York: Columbia University Press), pp. 19-52.

Kluckhohn, Clyde, 1949. *Mirror for Man* (New York: McGraw-Hill).

----------, and Leland C. Wyman, 1940. *An Introduction to Navaho Chant Practice,* American Anthropological Association Memoir 53 (Menasha, Wis.: George Banta).

Morgan, Lewis H., 1851. *League of the Ho-de-no-sau-nee, or Iroquois* (Rochester: Sage and Brother).

Oswalt, Wendell H., 1973. *This Land Was Theirs,* 2nd ed. (New York: John Wiley and Sons).

Parker, Arthur C., 1909. Secret Medicine Societies of the Seneca. *American Anthropologist* 11:161-185.

Sapir, Edward, 1949a. The Grammarian and His Language. In *Selected Writings of Edward Sapir,* David G. Mandelbaum, ed. (Berkeley: University of California Press), pp. 150-159.

----------, 1949b. The Unconscious Patterning of Behavior in Society. In *Selected Writings of Edward Sapir,* David G. Mandelbaum, ed. (Berkeley: University of California Press), pp. 544-559.

Shimony, Annemarie Anrod, 1961. *Conservatism among the Iroquois at the Six Nations Reserve,* Yale University Publications in Anthropology 65 (New Haven: Department of Anthropology, Yale University).

Speck, Frank G., 1949. *Midwinter Rites of the Cayuga Long House* (Philadelphia: University of Pennsylvania Press).

Titiev, Mischa, 1960. A Fresh Approach to the Problem of Magic and Religion. *Southwestern Journal of Anthropology* 16:292-298.

Tooker, Elisabeth, 1970. *The Iroquois Ceremonial of Midwinter* (Syracuse: University of Syracuse Press).

Tylor, Edward B., 1958. *Religion in Primitive Culture* (New York: Harper and Brothers). (Originally published in 1873 as chs. 11-19 of *Primitive Culture.*)

Wallace, Anthony F. C., 1966. *Religion: An Anthropological View* (New York: Random House).

Whorf, Benjamin Lee, 1956. Science and Linguistics. In *Language, Thought, and Reality: Selected Writings of Benjamin Lee Whorf,* John B. Carroll, ed. (New York: Wiley), pp. 207-219.

Belief in the Context of Rapid Change: An Eastern Cree Example

RICHARD J. PRESTON

TAKING an intellectual lead from Geertz in seeking to understand "the dynamic elements in social change which arise from the failure of cultural patterns to be perfectly congruent with the forms of social organization" (1957:33), this paper traces some aspects of ideological reinterpretation by Cree Indians on the east coast of James Bay, Canada. Our knowledge of belief systems in action for the eastern Subarctic area goes back to the Jesuit Relations of the early 1600's, and for James Bay itself, to the Hudson's Bay Company records beginning with Thomas Gorst's journal in 1670. The first post built by the company was at the mouth of the Rupert River, on James Bay, in 1668. And it is at this same location, now called Rupert House, that two contrasting cultural patterns have coalesced in the early 1970's, three hundred years later. These two patterns, both of them belief systems in action, are a Pentecostal church and an intra-culturally directed formal education program. They will be viewed in the context of their relevant historical antecedents, especially the reconstructed traditional baseline.

The embodiment of traditional Eastern Cree ideology in action has been detailed by Speck (1935), by myself (Preston 1971a), and by several others. I will only sketch and summarize here.

For the sake of clarity of exposition and appropriateness to the Cree data, I will use two perspectives on culture. The level of *private experience* refers to culture as it is actually experienced by its individual participants—culture as it is perceived and reflected upon by individual Cree persons. *Public participation* refers to culture as the interactions of persons, where each individual's private experience is, to varying degrees, embodied in actions vis-à-vis other persons. These two perspectives, the private or individual and the public or social, are complementary views of a single subject matter, in this case, Eastern Cree belief.

Traditional private experience for the Eastern Cree was set in the context of a hunter who was often very much dependent on his own resources in the solitary pursuit of game. Getting one's living meant finding and killing food in an arduous and sometimes unpredictable boreal forest environment. The requisite skills were demonstrated with marked emphasis on self-control, sensitivity to subtle cues and signs, fortitude, and resoluteness. Self-control is not only physical and cognitive, but also and importantly, emotional. An angry, jealous, anxious, or ecstatic man made a poor hunter, incapable of focusing his full attention on the task at hand (Preston 1971a).

Hunting songs intervened directly in the contingencies of getting a living, communicating to the animals one's deeply felt hope for success in hunting. An animal's reply might be perceived in the hunter's dreams and intuitions, and in the animal's significant actions (Preston 1970, 1971a). Competence in human activities was extended and facilitated by means of spiritual power. Some men sought to develop an individual relationship with an attending spirit (*Mistabeo*) perceived through dreams, intuitions, and significant experiences in daily activities. An individual's *Mistabeo* (literally "great man") normally assisted him by extending beyond human limits the effective actions of getting a living (by influencing food animals to expose their trails, influencing weather, curing illness, strengthening fortitude and hope, avoiding hazards of attack by alien groups or the covert attacks of sorcery, and so on).

In the sphere of public participation, the social aspect of traditional spiritual action is most notably illustrated by the conjuring tent ceremony. People did not gather to worship at the performances, but rather to see what a conjuror could do in communicating with his own *Mistabeo* and with the *Mistabeos* of individuals in other locations and with other spirit persons. The voices of all the spirits were clearly audible to the whole group, and the power of the spirits was indicated in the "shaking" or waving action of the barrel-shaped tent that contained only the conjuror and the spirits. As with the private relationship with the spirits described above, the goals were to extend human powers to intervene in life's contingencies. But here the benefits were usually extended to a social group, often consisting of the audience and perhaps some persons not present. Knowledge, power, and entertainment were blended in the conjuring act; the test of its value was empirical. If the knowledge proved valid, the power proved in action, the entertainment found admirable, then the conjuring was to that extent good.

Feasts were more simply social, a celebration of the human competence of the hunters, and reciprocally, of the generosity of the food-animals. At these times socializing included drumming and singing hunting or traveling songs to communicate thanks to the animals and to encourage the women and children to dance. They danced in a circular path, with relatively restrained movements. Feasts might celebrate some seasonal-cycle or life-cycle event, or simply the ample supply of meat from a big kill achieved either by an individual or a coordinated group hunting effort.

Hunting group leaders were selected on a case-by-case basis, each hunter voluntarily accepting temporary direction by a person of persuasive ecological, social, and spiritual competence. Henriksen's (1973) description of the Naskapi leadership pattern appears to fit the Eastern Cree pattern very well, except that the efforts of the Cree hunters are better described as coordinated. That is, rather than a cooperative division of tasks for a common goal, each hunter acted as an individual and noted his particular animals killed. The decision to share in a feast or in helping destitute persons was also individually made, although refusal to make the decision was unlikely. The significant cultural pattern here is a controlled responsibility for one's acts, in a group context as well as in individual situations.

The accumulative reinterpretive changes from the colonial period to the 1970's will be passed over very briefly.

The new technology introduced during the period both complicated and facilitated getting a living, but the attitudes toward coping were probably little changed, except as the physical dispersal necessary for trapping increased psychological individualism (Murphy and Steward 1956).

Songs were supplemented by hymns sung privately or publicly to communicate one's feelings to God, perhaps in the manner of the traditional songs.

God was integrated by some individuals as the spirit to whom the *Mistabeos* were answerable, by others as a more powerful replacement for *Mistabeo,* while others accepted the missionaries' discrediting of the *Mistabeo* as the Devil's manifestation.

In the domain of public participation, the Anglican Church provided a milieu for (coordinated?) group worship and encouraged "posting," the tendency for Indians to spend increasing amounts of time in the locale of the trading post and mission. The political stance of the Hudson's Bay Company "boss" was an authoritarian contrast to traditional leadership-by-example. His appointed "captains" directed some Indian men in "homeguard" activities, hunting for and otherwise serving the company traders, including arranging the seasonal canoe brigades that traveled to inland posts to exchange cargos of trade goods for fur. Beginning in the 1950's, additional church denominations, federal schools, and administrative personnel augmented the multi-ethnic character of the social organization of Rupert House, increasing some Indians' participation in wage labor, drinking, and welfare. Rupert House Cree have not viewed additional church denominations in the same way as have whites in the area. Whites tend to see a strong separation between different churches and their dogmas, while the Cree are inclined to view the differences as varying manifestations of a single domain of spiritual knowledge and action. People feel free to go to services at more than one church, and regard the admonitions of particular churchmen to be loyal to one denomination as the unnecessary narrowness of particular churchmen, not as decreed by God.

During the 1970-1974 period, the persistence of traditional belief remains strongs for many persons, but is sometimes weakly manifested. Others distort traditional beliefs in strongly reactive ways in response to the perceived pressures from outside for rapid and radical adaptation. A particularly dramatic stimulus is the multibillion dollar hydroelectric project that threatens to flood and otherwise alter the land, and to swamp (in an economic, social, and political sense) the communities with whites. The close integration of ecological, social, and spiritual aspects of both private experience and public participation are all blended in a general anticipation of calamity, "If the land goes, then the Indians go." More specific explanations of contemporary events in terms of old beliefs include the suggestions that forest fires in the vicinity of the main dam construction site were the result of conjuring against the project.

But more than explanation of hazardous events is involved. The hydro project has also stimulated motivations underlying contemporary ecological belief and action, and the more traditional hunter-trappers are now joined by others with a renewed interest in getting their living in the bush. I tentatively relate this renewal to new self-perception resulting from a wider context and a more critical view of white-dependent relationships, combined with the desire to protect something of great value that is threatened by the hydro project. Trapping, in its spiritual and social as well as ecological aspects, is no longer a dying art at Rupert House.

Traditional belief is also being reinterpreted in new situations. Secularization is most pronounced among some of the younger persons who have had formal education in residential schools in the south, pessimistically expressed in the title of a contemporary Ph.D. thesis, "From the Great Man [*Mistabeo*] to the White Man." But some of the consequences of secular belief have been positive and innovative. The prime example was the decision to take the hydro project to court, appealing to the law for control of both ecology and community. The results have been mixed, and litigation continues.

The most emotionally reactive case of beliefs in action took this anthropologist quite by surpise. In the summer of 1971 a Pentecostal church began holding meetings at Rupert House. The church was founded by a woman who returned to Rupert House at this time; she had shifted her residence and band membership to a more southerly locale some years before, after being one of the first women at Rupert House to be a "drinker." While the Holy Ghost ideas of Pentecostalism may parallel the traditional pattern of establishing a relationship with a *Mistabeo*, I doubt the importance to the leader of such a reinterpretation compared with the diffusionist alternative of learning Pentecostal belief while she actually observed and participated in the services held in the southern locale.

The overtly demonstrative emotional behavior (rhythmic loud singing, shouting, crying, dancing, falling down, speaking in tongues, and trance) that characterizes the meetings also has little precedent in traditional Cree terms, where self-control is markedly emphasized. Only behavior while drunk bears a limited comparison in my fieldwork experience. And significantly, of the seventeen hard core members, almost all are long-term drinkers in the thirty-to-fifty-year age range who have found Christian temperance in belief and behavior, without really giving up periods of intemperate (by Cree standards) emotional expression.

Also, significantly, most persons participating in both the earlier pattern of drinking and the later Pentecostalism have had restricted kinds of contact with white culture, largely through their jobs as service workers for local whites. None of the men involved make their living by hunting and trapping. Further, it is often the wives who lead their families into joining the Pentecostal group. Why the wives (and sometimes grown children) of men who have been superficially assimilating to white culture in the context of dependency on local white patrons should be the individuals to initiate membership remains a puzzle. Perhaps the movement will prove to be a transitional stage in moving cultural meanings toward a closer congruency with a more nearly white social organization. Yet I am more inclined to interpret these events as an ideological reaction to an unsatisfactory adaptation within an intercultural social organization. That is, by concentrating white belief and behavior into church services that are quite independent of white administration or participation, people feel they are in control of their own moral belief and actions. Less consciously, they set themselves toward both a white and an Indian standard of more respectable self-control in their out-of-church temperate behavior.

Although not formally members of a church, the adherents are closely knit in terms of ideological identity and in the actions most closely associated with their Pentecostal ideology. The most obvious area of ·action, the service itself, commonly lasts four to six hours, usually on consecutive days. The Bible is interpreted with regard to prohibitions of sinful behavior, notably drinking, card-playing, and even the operation of skidoos in the vicinity of a service since the noise interferes with the proceedings. Testimony on miraculous manifestations of faith and power may refer to success in coping with rather ordinary contingencies in everyday life, such as refusing medications as a cure for sickness, or traveling safely through rough weather on a plane. To date there have been three predictions of doomsday, the most recent prediction being for April 8, 1974.

The church has introduced some new hazards into the community. When a second family moved from the southern locale's Pentecostal group to Rupert House, the leader's actions became more demonstrative and emotional as she apparently felt her leadership threatened; she gossiped harshly to others that the new woman's face was turning black, because of the Devil. Also socially hazardous is the disinclination of members to associate with nonmembers.

In contexts removed from the services, actions guided by belief center on temperance behavior and the avoidance of relationships with nonbelievers. The markedly reduced drinking by adherents prompted some non-Pentecostals to regard the new church with curiosity and some tolerance. But the tolerance is now wearing thin, since the exclusiveness of the group, their gossip's blatant aggressiveness, their marked lack of tolerance, seemingly contrived or "acted out" behavior, and lack of mature competence in both Cree and white terms has put a strain on many nonbelievers' patience and acceptance. Finally, Pentecostals have expressed their support for the hydro project, saying that the Eskimos (and by implication, some much closer Indian neighbors!) ought to have something done to them because they are against the hydro.

The degree to which Pentecostalism is, for its members at Rupert House, a reinterpretation of old belief and behavior can only be suggested here. If self-control seems lacking in church services, certainly it is regained in the narrow areas of behavior covered by temperance, and each individual speaks and acts responsibly for himself. Testimonials provide dramatic oratory of spiritual intervention in events. The lack of formal membership or authority is consistent with tradition. In the area of private experience, spiritual power, songs, and coping with empirical contingencies are still well united. In the area of public participation, church services, generous cash contributions (analogous to traditional food contributions at a feast), leadership through persuasion, and coordinated group efforts for ecological coping (supporting the hydro project for economic opportunity) may be noted. In spite of these parallels, the Pentecostal movement is substantially an imported pattern of belief and behavior that exhibits a negative and reactive emotional pattern characteristic of a particular subgroup of Rupert House society.

In support of this argument, we may note that Pentecostalism in Rupert House shares standardized attributes found in other northern native Pentecostal groups. For example, Clairmont (1963:39-44) has described a similar situation for Aklavik, led by Eskimo persons and participated in by Indians. Closer to James Bay, Rogers and Black (personal communications) have told me of a very similar group at Round Lake, Ontario. At Round Lake, as at Rupert House, a person who had left the community and gone to a place where Pentecostalism was already active returned and became a leader of a local group.

More than a century ago, temperance movements had been the Algonkian response to stress and an alternative to the Ghost Dance; some details of two cases are described by Mooney (1896:705-706). All of these cases appear to fit the general definition by LaBarre (1970: chs. 1-5) of a crisis cult, a reactive and heavily irrational grasping for spiritual power and security in response to the felt stresses of intercultural pressures for apparently unachieveable change.

But Geertz (1966) offers a more precise theoretical explanation. In his definition of religion as a cultural system one can find logical relations to explain particular cases. In these terms, Pentecostal belief acts to set moods and motives of spiritual election (where the Holy Spirit chooses to enter a person), temperance and righteousness in preparation for doomsday, when believers will triumph over all worldly difficulties. Members give manifest support to these beliefs, moods, and motives through the ritual of church services and through the unique testament of miracles that gives a special quality of reality to their world.

In an earlier case study quoted at the beginning of this paper, Geertz (1957) describes the impetus given to change when there is a discontinuity between cultural meanings and social organization. In the Rupert House setting, reactive ideological changes are an attempt to cope with the frustrations of an unsuccessful intercultural adaptation. I will contrast this with a more positive, innovative, proactive (Murray 1959) combination of belief and action. The innovation concerns an intraculturally directed formal education system described in the following section.

Another significant shift of residence took place in the summer of 1971, when a woman who was the first high school graduate from the Rupert House Band moved back to live on the east coast of the bay. Her husband was a teacher and had obtained his first principalship at the Paint Hills school about one hundred miles north of Rupert House. From their arrival, they sought with appropriate actions to integrate themselves with the other Indian families of the community, based on the belief that both their role as family and as school administrator should be responsive to, and integral with, the community. Since teachers and, more notably, school principals have traditionally associated with and been responsive to the white enclave in these communties, the innovation of this family was quite significant. The new principal's behavior was also unusually competent in Cree terms since he avoided authoritarian attitudes and actions, preferring to make the school's program responsible to the local band council. He urged teachers to visit the children's families socially and advised on how they might make their classroom roles more suitable for acceptance and respect by the children. The community response was positive and supportive. When the government refused funding for a bush camp, where skills might be taught as a part of the curriculum, parents volunteered and built the camp. Absenteeism dropped markedly and remained low. Adult classes were filled and stayed filled.

The bush camp experience was supplemented by mimeographed readers and workbooks based on remembered history, belief, and technical knowledge of hunting and trapping, and gradually this cultural content was put more into terms of Cree semantic and behavioral structures. At the end of the second year, the Band Council at Rupert House asked for and obtained the transfer of the principal from Paint Hills to their school with the purpose of achieving similar integration of school and community. The past year has seen substantial progress toward this goal.

The beliefs relating to the intracultural education program are, in schematic form: (1) that primary education should begin by meeting the resources of the particular children—what they bring to school in terms of prior experience and skills, (2) that both the structure and content of education continue in this intracultural fashion, only gradually and in a planned curriculum, grading into a more cosmopolitan or intercultural education, and (3) that the more cosmopolitan goals of education can best be served when based on a solid background of intracultural competence.

Extra-community actions resulting from these beliefs include the granting by the Department of Indian Affairs of a band petition for full band control of grades K, 1, 2, and 3 for the fall of 1974. A low-profile kind of action anthropology on my part has included obtaining a grant from a private foundation of $70,000 over a three-year period to pay the costs of the education program's project to collect and produce Indian curriculum materials. These external actions have helped to confirm the possibility of realizing the need felt within the community for community-based education. Many individuals (almost all in the over-thirty age range) have committed themselves to work on the project, and a voluntary association of coordinated individuals has developed across religious boundaries (Pentecostal included) and with expressions of support from much of the community. In the opinion of the principal, the project offers a constructive alternative to Pentecostalism, and has developed a lively moral sense that seems to be accompanied by some quieting down of the Pentecostal fervor.

The degree to which the intracultural education program is, for the community members at Rupert House, a reinterpretation of old belief and behavior may be taken on more than one level. The structure, form, and content of the envisaged curriculum aim explicitly at this goal (the interpretation, for children, of traditional Cree life). Once the goal is achieved, it will become the intracultural base on which a later intercultural curriculum can be most adaptively constructed. But it is at the level of the project itself, rather than its envisaged product, that I presently wish to examine belief and action.

Because each individual participates in the project on an entirely voluntary basis and with his own reasons for choosing what he does, the perspective of private experience is particularly appropriate to this data. As with hunting for a living, where self-control facilitates proactive mustering of one's inner resources to direct technical, social, and mental skills, individuals who are working on the education project as researchers, technicians, or resource persons share an attitude (or mood and motive) that is not a reaction to anxiety, anger, or cynicism, but rather an attempt to cope as successfully as possible with a contemporary social and cultural environment. Most of these individuals are over thirty and competent in their family role as hunter-trappers or wives. The native-language teachers are younger, but qualified by a combination of formal education and ability in the bush. Their background of personal experience, then, fits them for their particular tasks. Individuals working on the project repeatedly manifest attention to detail and to probing the limits of available resources. The spiritual aspect is not likely to include relationships with animal or spiritual persons, but a heartfelt hope for success in their immediate and long-range goals has motivated a surprising quantity and quality of work completed to date, much of it having great ethnographic interest.

At the level of public participation, action is partly coordinated, partly cooperative. Each individual works independently on his understood tasks, but with a community goal and with some cooperative specialization. Persons collecting information or specimens of technology check in with the principal only once in a few days, insure that the further needs are understood, and return to their own individual efforts. Since the nature of the materials is well known to them, and the understanding of purpose and priority is well shared, they have accumulated a rich store of raw materials. At an open house held recently, all the community was invited to have a look at what the project has produced so far.

Band council support has included petitioning Indian Affairs for control of levels K, 1, 2, and 3, and endorsing the project. The school principal has combined the "whiteman" role of field supervisor of the grant and primary executive for the entire project, with the more Cree attributes of a coordinator through persuasive leadership without assertive ego-identification. One might well characterize the result as a charismatic project without dependence on a charismatic leader. Similar persuasive leadership directs the style of the native teachers in their relationships to the children, and of course also characterizes the parent-child relationship in the family setting. This consistency in the style of social relationships is deliberate and appropriate, and makes for minimum discontinuity for the children as school gives way to vacations for whole families to go on the spring goose hunts, and accommodates other family-centered enculturative experiences that are integrated with the in-school curriculum.

Volunteer consultants from the fields of education, linguistics, psychology, and anthropology who share an enthusiasm for the goals and means of the project provide intercultural expertise. Their work is currently coordinated to assist in the preparation of scheduled and easily utilized curriculum materials that native teachers can use, in Cree and in English, with ease and consistency and only a minimum of direct guidance from the principal, and without training in a teacher's college or formal teaching experience. During the summer of 1974, the teachers, principal, and consultants plan to gather at Manitou Community College for the working out of materials and procedures in anticipation of the beginning of the curriculum in the fall.

Recognition of the discontinuity between Cree enculturation and the formal education given to Cree children during the past twenty-five years as well as the discontinuity between the knowledge and values of formally educated Cree and the actual social organization of the home community has led to a plan to alter the educational ex-perience to better fit the social milieu of the community. The program aspires to more, however. It aims at a planned grading into intercul-tural educational experience in order to facilitate present and future intercultural adaptations, either within the community or beyond it.

I have noted two cases of discontinuity between contemporary cultural meanings (private experience) and social organization (public participation); both discontinuities are products in some way of in-tercultural influences on intracultural patterns.

One case relates to Cree who are no longer hunter-trappers, but rather have been engaged in wage work as service laborers for local whites, and subsequently have turned to Pentecostalism. The new religious persuasion is strongly reactive, much more dramatically so than I thought possible three years ago when I predicted (Preston 1971b) something comparable to the adoption of Alcoholics Anonymous reported by Steinbring (1968) for the Lake Winnipeg Ojibwa.

Pentecostal beliefs are embodied in action (beyond the church services) that adapts social organization to serve the particular felt needs of a superficially assimilated subgroup within the intercultural Rupert House society. The behavior provides a basis for clearly defining the subgroup and legitimizing it in the temperate action that is con-sistent with both Cree and white traditional values. Yet in the very acts defining subgroup boundaries, these persons show an intolerant exclusivity that has made acceptance by the rest of the community difficult. Non-Pentecostals find that the essentially reactive, self-serving attributes of Pentecostalism result in actions that either lack control (in the church services) or lack social acceptance of the community (outside of the church services).

The second case illustrates a proactive (action guided more by individuals' inner resources than by external pressures) attempt at a resolution of the discontinuity between cultural meanings and social organization. Formal education, in both its pedagogical structure and its semantic structure, has presented a generation of Cree children with a domain of white cultural meanings. The white cultural meanings are discontinuous not only with those of the Rupert House children who are entering school, but also with the social organization of the community. The difficulty is more clearly and explicitly understood than in the Pentecostal case, and the adaptive course excludes no one with regard to participation or with regard to goals. Intracommunity belief and action aims at unanimous participation, whether directly as researchers, resource persons, teachers, students, parents or, less directly, simply as understanding and supportive community members. Educational goals proceed from the relatively exclusive intracultural structure and content, as the children are able to deal competently with more cosmopolitan educational objectives, to intercultural educational structure and content.

Education beliefs are embodied in action (beyond the school classes) that adapts social organization to serve the felt needs of the community to improve formal education of the children, so that going to school will not create a superficially assimilated subgroup that finds difficulty in reintegrating with the home community.

Curiously, neither case utilizes traditional Cree forms of songs, dreams and intuitions, or spirit persons, although these ideological aspects persisted prominently in the past. The Pentecostal group participates in the songs and spirit of a white Christian sect, and the education project is fundamentally secular, objectifying particular old beliefs as a respected part of the content of curriculum more than taking them with faith as an integral part of one's private experience.

REFERENCES

Clairmont, D. H. J., 1963. *Deviance among Indians and Eskimos in Aklavik, N.W.T.,* Northern Co-ordination and Research Centre, NCRC-63-6 (Ottawa: Department of Indian Affairs and Northern Development).

Geertz, Clifford, 1957. Ritual and Social Change: A Javanese Example. *American Anthropologist* 59:32-54.

————, 1966. Religion As a Cultural System. In *Anthropological Approaches to the Study of Religion,* M. Banton, ed. (London: Tavistock Publications), pp. 1-46.

Henriksen, Georg, 1973. *Hunters in the Barrens* (St. John's, Newfoundland: Institute of Social and Economic Research, Memorial University of Newfoundland).

LaBarre, Weston, 1970. *The Ghost Dance* (New York: Doubleday).

Mooney, James, 1896. *The Ghost Dance Religion.* In *Fourteenth Annual Report of the Bureau of American Ethnology* (Washington, D.C.: Government Printing Office), pt. 2.

Murphy, R., and J. Steward, 1956. Tappers and Trappers: Parallel Processes in Acculturation. *Economic Development and Cultural Change* 4:335-353.

Murray, H. A., Jr., 1959. Preparation for the Scaffold of a Comprehensive

System. In *Psychology: A Study of a Science,* S. Koch, ed., vol. 3 (New York: McGraw-Hill), pp. 8-56.

Preston, Richard J., 1970. On the Relationships between Human Persons and Food-animal Persons. (Paper read at the Third Conference on Algonquian Studies, Trent University, Peterborough, Ontario.)

————, 1971a. Cree Narration: An Expression of the Personal Meanings of Events. (Ph.D. diss., Department of Anthropology, University of North Carolina.)

————, 1971b. Problèmes humains reliés au développement de la Baie James. *Recherches amérindiennes au Québec* 1:58-68. (English-language copy available from author.)

Speck, Frank G., 1935. *Naskapi: The Savage Hunters of the Labrador Peninsula* (Norman: University of Oklahoma Press).

Steinbring, Jack, 1968. Acculturational Phenomena among the Lake Winnipeg Ojibwa of Canada. In *Verhandlungen des XXXVIII Internationalen Amerikanistenkongresses,* Bd. 3 (Munich: Klaus Renner), pp. 179-188.

Belief System, Millenary Expectations, and Behavior

Felicitas D. Goodman

The topic of the symposium charges us with the task of considering the articulation of belief system and behavior. Articulation to me suggests an anatomical simile, namely the manner in which bones are joined, the ball-and-socket design of the femur with the hip, for instance. The problem with this analogy is, however, that the ball and the socket are structures on the same level, so to speak. They join bone to bone, i.e., equivalent sections of the skeleton. The same statement cannot be made of behavior and belief system. Behavior is open to direct observation, but a belief system is not immediately accessible to scrutiny. To discover what an informant's belief system might be, we have to rely on his statements, his introspection, as well as on observations of his behavior. In addition, not even the informant himself is aware of the entire body of his beliefs, much of which is hidden from awareness for all of us. We are thus asked to speak of the relationships between an overt system, namely behavior, and a covert system, the discovery of which may be quite difficult.

When speaking about culture as behavior, Arensberg (1972) suggests a scheme where ethnographic data are translated into regular recurrences of specified interpersonal coactions. A highly consistent representation can in this manner be generated for such macrophenomena as kinship systems, market behavior, and others purely from observed interpersonal events. I imagine that it would be an attractive task to generate the nomenclature—as does Arensberg for kinship—for, say, the religion of a particular society from sequencing the recurrent behavioral regularities in that society. But what if we have to represent change? Whether Arensberg's model would be powerful enough to cope with the tremendous task of reordering a large number of variables, many of them not even known because of being part of a covert system, is a question as yet to be tested.

Wallace (1970:32ff.) maintains that we cannot say anything about what is in the mind, what he calls the "cognitive map," but can participate only in "secondary equivalence structures," i.e., behavior, when the individual interacts in society. I might spin this further by saying that in situations of change, we might see evidence that modifications are introduced into the cognitive map that alter the secondary equivalence structure, producing distortions in societal interaction because behavior can no longer be reliably predicted.

The question remains, however, of *how* a new trait is introduced into the cognitive map and by what mechanism it changes the secondary equivalence structure. Wallace does speak to this subject when he considers the psychological process taking place in revitalization movements (1966), in becoming a shaman, and in cultural innovation generally (1970). Calling it mazeway resynthesis, he defines the process as "a rather sudden reorganization . . . of values, attitudes, and beliefs that 'make sense' of a hitherto confusing and anxiety-provoking world" (1970:237). Wallace suggests, then, that values, attitudes, and beliefs are themselves reshuffled. But how? Is it entirely helter-skelter, obeying only the instruction, "make sense"? Given the highly systematic nature of human mental processes, I would answer in the negative. In fact, I would go so far as to suggest that far from reshuffling values, attitudes, and beliefs haphazardly, what really happens in the shamanistic and other, similar experiences of cultural innovation is the introduction of new rules, leaving the underlying structure more or less undisturbed.

As is obvious from this line of argument, I am applying a linguistic model. Some criticism against this procedure has recently been advanced. Thus, in a recent article, Bohannan (1973:359) warns against the use of an analogy with language, calling it a definitional ploy, and the most confusing one at that. I would agree with him if by analogical use of language he means such explanatory schemes as the analogy of culture traits with minimal units of meaning or morphs, for instance, or the analogy of the scheme of social interaction with grammar. This I do not propose to do. In fact, I do not want to use analogical reasoning at all. I do not want to say that the culture change in the millenary cult described below proceeded just like language change, for instance. Rather, I am convinced with Noam Chomsky (1972:viii) that "the study of language structure reveals properties of mind that underlie the exercise of human mental capacities in normal activities, such as the use of language in ordinary free and creative fashion."

One of the properties of mind that Noam Chomsky discusses in some detail in his various publications about transformational, generative grammar (see e.g., 1965a, 1965b) is the availability to the speaker of a linguistic "deep structure." A number of transformational rules are applied to a given content of this deep structure, giving rise to the actual communicated, perceivable "surface structure." I should like to demonstrate in this paper that the post-upheaval phase of a crisis cult in Yucatán can be accounted for in a very satisfactory way by referring to this "property of mind," in order to analyze a particular "exercise of human mental capacities." To accomplish such an analysis, I want to call "deep structure" those capabilities of a person, largely hidden, which constitute Wallace's "cognitive map." Marvin Harris (1968:455) describes this area of personality as follows: "It is perfectly obvious that each individual contains within himself resources, potentialities, inhibitions, and anxieties in multitudes and varieties far beyond the manifest content of actual, momentary existence." As we know from cross-cultural enculturation studies, this "cultural deep structure" is fixed early in life. We probably are dealing here with the same neurophysiological maturation process linguists have encountered in studies on language acquisition (Carol Chomsky 1969). Lenneberg summarizes his research results in this area:

> Between the ages of three and the early teens the possibility for early language acquisition continues to be good; the individual appears to be most sensitive to stimuli at this time and to preserve some innate flexibility for the organization of brain functions. . . . After puberty, the ability for self-organization . . . quickly declines. The brain behaves as if it had become set in its ways. (1967:158)

The transformational rules operating on the deep structure are derived from culturally accepted norms of behavior and generate the surface structure of actual, perceivable behavior. I would propose that while the deep structure remains in the main unchanged, new transformational rules may be added or subtracted during an individual's lifetime in a continuous adjustment to changing circumstances. Religious conversion represents such a rule change, as I should like to demonstrate in the following account.

Pentecostal missionizing spread to Mexico early this century represented predominantly by the Apostolic denomination. The Yucatecan peninsula became the target of these efforts in 1959. Proselytizing was more successful in the rural areas of Yucatán than in the few urban centers. In the towns, the sect spread mainly via contact between neighbors; its propagation in the villages followed a different pattern. Almost exclusively, peasant men and women with a history of religious experimentation came in contact with some Apostolic evangelist in one of the urban centers of Yucatán and carried the discovery of a new religious style back to their home villages, where the formation of small congregations then proceeded along the kinship network.

The Apostolic congregation of Utzpak,[1] where I did fieldwork, was also formed in this manner. From the start, thus, there were two different types of members in the group. There were first of all the innovators, who had previously examined various other religious possibilities, such as those offered by the Presbyterians, the Baptists, Jehovah's Witnesses, and others and had decided on their own to give the Apostolic approach a try. And there were the followers, who had been recruited into the experiment by kin, as the most accessible to the missionizing effort of the innovators within the larger village community where visiting patterns predominantly involve kin.

We are justified, I think, to consider the innovator-follower distinction as one of deep structure. However, the deep structure, as shown by field observation, contained also other elements relevant to this analysis. In the 1960's and early 1970's, the peasant population of this Maya village—and probably of many Indian villages of the Latin American world generally—was by no means homogeneous, and this was reflected in the congregation. Within the incipient class structure of the village, there was the lower class and the more affluent, less traditional upper class.[2] In addition, there was a generational feature, distinguishing the somewhat older, established villagers from the restless young exposed from early childhood to radio, some television, and much visiting to the market of the state capital because of the new paved highway and the bus service instituted in the 1960's. Each group also possessed a mobility factor built into the area of social aspirations within the deep structure. The lower-class individual pressed toward the upper-class status within the village, the upper class toward urban lifestyles, and the restless rural young within the same urban aspiration yearned for adventure, glow, and glamour. For economic reasons, mainly because young women—unlike young men— can find jobs in the city as domestics and sales personnel, the restless young rural group consisted entirely of girls. The young men, their age mates, belonged to the lower class in the above classification.

Keeping these various elements of the deep structure in mind, it becomes entirely understandable why the clergy coming from the city and representing urban lifeways and sophistication is generally more successful in these village congregations than are peasant pastors. Served mostly by preachers risen from their own ranks, the Apostolic congregation in Utzpak more or less stagnated until 1969, when it received a minister who was born and raised in Campeche, the second-largest town of the Peninsula. This man was an excellent speaker as well as a knowledgeable guide into the trance behavior and the ritual of speaking in tongues.[3] Under his tutelage, the congregation increased rapidly, reaching its peak the following year with about eighty adult members.

The dogma of the Apostolic Church demands a renunciation of the pleasures of the world such as committing adultery, dancing, smoking, drinking, going to picture shows, and wearing jewelry. All members believe in the need for adult baptism with water to wash away accumulated sins and create a new person. At first glance it may seem odd that such an "unworldly" dogma should attract people involved in the very "worldly" aspirations I maintained above. But the choice becomes understandable in terms of the model that I suggested. The converts, in this case, were not altering anything in their deep structure, but only adopting a new transformational rule. The rule is one of the simplest to apply, and is known to linguists as a "flip-flop rule."

The rule merely gives the instruction that whatever the former ways of behavior might have been, the opposite is now to be prescribed. The converts, applying the rule within the narrow domain of church doctrine, now adopted a divinely sanctioned lifestyle antithetical to their former ways. The above "worldly" goals of mobility remained entirely intact in the deep structure, however. How precarious the institution of a new transformational rule is and how easily the work of conversion can be undone on the basis of a "late-in, early-out" mechanism, is evidenced by much anguished preaching in these churches against backsliding. This is, of course, entirely in keeping with Lenneberg's neurophysiological view that after puberty, the brain is set in its ways, and less capable of self-organization.

The ritual of speaking in tongues is a central new behavior in the Pentecostal movement but it cannot, I propose, be subsumed under the flip-flop rule. Speaking in tongues, or glossolalia, is not simply nonsense language, i.e., the opposite of a natural language (Goodman 1972). It is the manifestation of an entirely different deep structure, namely, that of the highly aroused altered mental state, and is not the result of the instruction, "formerly you spoke in intelligible language, now you don't." The experience of an altered mental state and the interpretation that glossolalia represents a possession by the Holy Spirit acquainted the congregation with a radically new religious experience, the perception of direct, personal, overwhelming contact with the supernatural.[4] The importance of the new minister of the Utzpak congregation as the guide into this new, intoxicating human range cannot be overestimated.

I have detailed elsewhere (Goodman 1973, 1974a) the events of the crisis cult that broke out in the congregation in the summer of 1970. Briefly, some members of the congregation began to hallucinate, and the content of these hallucinations was interpreted as indicating that the end of the world was imminent. Prayer meetings were held night and day, the ordinary structure of the worship service dissolved, making place for greatly extended sessions with speaking in tongues and interpreting these tongues as messages from the Holy Spirit concerning the end of the world. Colored clothing and other colored articles of possession were burned. A number of men went on an evangelizing crusade to convert the rest of the world in order to save as many people as possible from the destruction to come. The women left at home started living communally and all property and income was to be shared.

The triggering mechanism for the cult was, in my mind, a change in the minister's behavior. His life history showed a tendency toward easy enthusiasm and subsequent withdrawal from commitments to various causes. In the early months of 1970, as his enthusiasm for his mission in Utzpak began to fade, he experienced considerable culture shock as a result of his life in a peasant community, and he began rejecting the congregation. The congregation, in turn, reacted with panic, mingled with aggression. Since they had recently and *as a group* been taught to utilize highly excited altered mental states, this group trance acted to intensify, enormously to magnify this reaction. If we take into consideration that simultaneously, in such trance states, there is also a lowering of inhibitions, it becomes understandable that the abandonment experience of the congregation led it to introduce a new transformational rule at this point of the evolution of the cult. This rule contained the instruction, "destroy the social order." The millenary expectation about the Lord's bringing about the end of the world is thus actually a self-fulfilling prophecy in the sense that it voices the intent of the congregation. Applying this rule, therefore, the congregation proceeded to dissolve the ritual structure of the worship service, subverted the role of the minister, and sullied the temple; in the personal sphere, they burned property, abolished the family, and proclaimed their willingness to die. It is most illuminating for the relationship between social process and the physiological condition of trance that when the latter dissolved, while the crisis cult continued, the introduction and application of the rule concerning the destruction of the social order was interpreted as having been the result of satanic possession.

At the end of August 1970 the trance behavior, i.e., the physiological phenomenon, ceased; the congregation, one might say, woke up. The many innovations introduced into the culture of the group in pursuance of the transformational rule concerning the destruction of the social order disappeared, indicating that the transformational rule itself, with a "last-in, last-out" command, had been completely rubbed out.

In the course of the subsequent two years, the congregation of Utzpak as well as other congregations that had participated in the upheaval split into four descendant groups. All four of them shared the decision to close the door on the altered mental state as supernaturally too dangerous (Goodman 1974b). But while all four groups had lost the rule about the destruction of the social order, all four applied the flip-flop rule to devise newly sanctioned behavior.

Three of the four groups preserved a religious life. A reference to the deep structure components outlined above, as well as to the roles the groups played in their community, will make clear why this should be so. The innovators remained within the Apostolic Church. Most of them had come to the denomination on the basis of an intellectual decision, much discussed in the larger community. They had been members of the congregation for a number of years, had helped build the temple. The role expected of them as Apostolics in the larger village community as much as their own habits kept them within that structure. Most of the members recruited through kinship slipped away to two new sects. These were the persons who had been identified most strongly with the belief in the imminent end of the world, and responding to social pressure within the village, they had to stay within this role. One of these groups linked up with a missionizing effort originating in the United States. Publicized by the *Spoken Word* publications, this sect proclaims that William Marrion Branham, a revivalist preacher (died in 1965) was the new prophet of the Lord. The end of the world would come after San Francisco was destroyed by an earthquake and the Third World War had broken out. The other group was recruited by a native Maya evangelist, Don Venancio.[5] Expelled from the Apostolic Church because of his deviating theological views, he continues to claim that the end of the world is near, but the point in time cannot be calculated exactly because man's time and God's time are not identical.

The most interesting of the four groups is the one of the young girls. They had conceived of urbanization in terms of a new, fascinating sex role. Aiming at urban patterns through the minister, they saw in him a powerful sexual attraction. When he withdrew and, some time after the dissolution of the crisis cult, deserted the congregation, their entire involvement with the church collapsed, and they went on to other sexual attractions. In a recursive application of the flip-flop rule, they negated all tenets of their Apostolic faith and returned to worldly ways. The recursive application of the flip-flop rule is most evident in the way they married. They either chose men unacceptable to the congregation on religious grounds, or they married the native way, "being robbed," i.e., without benefit of clergy or public registry, anathema to the Apostolics.

Viewed in one way, all members of the congregation that went through the cycle of millenary expectations lost something. After all, the end of the world did not come, and they all suffered from ridicule and from an upsetting of their lifeways. Yet from the point of view of the social aspirations built into their deep structure, they all emerged as winners. The conservative group that stuck to the temple and the members who attached themselves to Don Venancio were all trying to move to the upper bracket of village society. They in fact accomplished this by the status they acquired as innovators. Of the kin-recruited members, those with urban aspirations broke into an intensely urban, American-oriented sect, and one family at least moved to the urban center of Chetumal. Members belonging initially to the village upper class assumed a more urban lifestyle and became preachers, renting their small ranches to peasants and gaining in prestige by assuming a different, intellectual role.

Conversion experience, Wallace (1970) and others have maintained, involves a deep-going change in personality structure. If at all, this will, however, be true only in the most exceptional cases. The prolonged observation of and intimate acquaintance with a single innovative congregation, reflected in the above discussion, shows that culture change at most calls for the introduction of some new transformational rule, applied, and subsequently quite often discarded, to serve the individual's needs. Such a view may account for the conservative and ponderous nature of most culture change.

NOTES

The field research for this paper was carried out intermittently from 1969 to 1973 with the help of summer grants from the Denison University Faculty Development Fund.

[1]Names of persons and places are changed to protect the privacy of the individuals involved.

[2]The lower-upper dichotomy in the incipient village class structure does not take into consideration the "rich," a stratum only marginally rural and not integrated for economic reasons into the range of aspirations of the rural population. The village upper class, seen from an urban perspective, would be ranged in the lower-middle class.

[3]For details on this speech behavior, see Goodman 1972.

[4]For a discussion of culture and altered mental states, see Bourguignon 1973 and 1974.

[5]A pseudonym.

REFERENCES

Arensberg, Conrad M., 1972. Culture as Behavior. *Annual Review of Anthropology* 1:1-26.

Bohannan, Paul, 1973. Rethinking Culture: A Project for Current Anthropologists. *Current Anthropology* 14:357-372.

Bourguignon, Erika, ed., 1973. *Religion, Altered States of Consciousness, and Social Change* (Columbus: Ohio State University Press).

----------, 1974. *Culture and the Varieties of Consciousness.* An Addison-Wesley Module in Anthropology, No. 47 (Reading, Mass.: Addison-Wesley).

Chomsky, Carol, 1969. *The Acquisition of Syntax in Children from 5 to 10.* Research Monograph No. 57 (Cambridge, Mass.: M.I.T. Press).

Chomsky, Noam, 1965a. *Aspects of the Theory of Syntax* (Cambridge, Mass.: M.I.T. Press).

----------, 1965b. *Syntactic Structures* (The Hague: Mouton).

----------, 1972. *Language and Mind.* Enlarged edition (New York: Harcourt, Brace, Jovanovich).

Goodman, Felicitas D., 1972. *Speaking in Tongues: A Cross-Cultural Study of Glossolalia* (Chicago: University of Chicago Press).

----------, 1973. The Apostolics of Yucatán: A Case Study of a Religious Movement. In *Religion, Altered States of Consciousness, and Social Change,* Erika Bourguignon, ed. (Columbus: Ohio State University Press), pp. 178-218.

----------, 1974a. Disturbances in the Apostolic Church: A Trance-Based Upheaval in Yucatán. In *Trance, Healing, and Hallucination: Three Field Studies in Religious Experience,* by Felicitas D. Goodman, Jeannette H. Henney, and Esther Pressel (New York: Wiley-Interscience), pp. 227-364.

----------, 1974b. Not to Speak in Tongues: Abstention from Glossolalia in a Yucatecan Crisis Cult. (Paper prepared for the session on "Sociology of Language and Religion," Eighth World Congress of Sociology, Toronto, Canada, August 1974.)

Harris, Marvin, 1968. *The Rise of Anthropological Theory* (New York: Crowell).

Lenneberg, Eric H., 1967. *Biological Foundations of Language* (New York: Wiley).

Wallace, Anthony F. C., 1966. *Religion: An Anthropological View* (New York: Random).

----------, 1970. *Culture and Personality,* 2nd ed. (New York: Random).

The Contributors

Michael V. Angrosino is assistant professor of anthropology at the University of South Florida in Tampa. His major interests are in medical anthropology and community health planning. His research includes studies of alcoholism therapy in Trinidad, West Indies, and of home care services for the aged in Florida.

Clifford Geertz is professor of social science at the Institute for Advanced Study, Princeton, New Jersey. His major interests are social change, symbol systems, and the theory of culture. He has done fieldwork in Indonesia and Morocco.

Felicitas D. Goodman is assistant professor of anthropology and linguistics at Denison University, Granville, Ohio. She is interested mainly in religious behavior, especially as it relates to altered states of consciousness; in peasant studies; and in culture change in the Latin American area. She started her fieldwork in Yucatán in 1969, and is continuing it to date in an effort to develop a longitudinal study of the evolution of a revitalization movement.

Carole E. Hill is assistant professor of anthropology at Georgia State University. She has also been appointed assistant professor in the School of Urban Life. Her major interests are belief systems, anthropological theory, medical anthropology, and complex societies. Having carried out field research in Costa Rica and the American south, she is currently studying the adaptive problems of ethnic groups in Atlanta.

Charles Hudson is associate professor of anthropology at the University of Georgia. His main interests are in the Indians of the southeastern United States and in folk belief systems. He is author of *The Catawba Nation* and *The Southeastern Indians* and editor of *Red, White, and Black: Symposium on Indians in the Old South* and *Four Centuries of Southern Indians*.

Frank E. Manning is assistant professor of anthropology at Memorial

University of Newfoundland, St. John's. His major field research has dealt with both religious and secular symbol systems in Bermuda, Barbados, and Antigua. He has also done a study of social problems and interpersonal tensions aboard oceanographic research ships.

James L. Peacock is professor of anthropology, University of North Carolina, Chapel Hill. His primary interests are in psychological and symbolic anthropology, and he has done field work in Southeast Asia and North Carolina.

Richard J. Preston is associate professor of anthropology at McMaster University in Hamilton, Ontario. His major research interests include the persistence of traditional ideology, and contemporary educational problems and solutions. He has conducted repeated field research with the Eastern Cree as part of a long-term study of Cree cultural and social change.

Elisabeth Tooker is associate professor of anthropology at Temple University, Philadelphia. Her major interests are the religion and social organization of the North American Indians, particularly the Iroquois.

Victor W. Turner is professor of social thought and of anthropology at the University of Chicago. He has done fieldwork among the Ndembu and Lamba of Zambia and the Gisu of Uganda and has collected data on pilgrimage processes in Mexico, Ireland, England, and France. His major interests are in symbolic action, ritual, and anthropological approaches to intercivilizational processes. He is the author of *Schism and Continuity in an African Society, The Forest of Symbols, The Drums of Affliction, The Ritual Process,* and *Dramas, Fields and Metaphors.*

My eye has shaped my hands
And hands my feet:
My bones and sinews whisper.
They sing of my ancient clap
Ancient ways.
Throat, tongue
    to sing my feet to dance
    and hands to clap